Training from the Neck Up: A practical guide to sport psychology for riders

April Clay, M.Ed., Chartered Psychologist

A complete mental training manual for amateur and professional riders

Published by The Writing Room
5477 Patina Drive SW
Calgary, Alberta, Canada T3H 3J8

Canadian Cataloging in Publication Data
Clay, April, 1966-
Training From the Neck Up:
A Practical Guide to Sport Psychology for Riders
Includes bibliographical references
ISBN 0-9685822-0-6
1. Horsemanship-Psychological Aspects I. Title
SF295.2.C53 1999   782.2'01'9   C99-901094-8

Cover and illustrations by Andrew LeMessurier

First Edition

Acknowledgments

*I would like to thank my illustrator and partner,
Andrew LeMessurier, for his assistance,
inspiration and support.
Thanks Andy.*

Contents:

Introduction

Your greatest aid on a horse is your brain
-George Morris

I distinctly remember attending one George Morris clinic where he posed this question: "what is your most important aid on a horse?" Predictably, we all smugly yelled responses like: "legs!", "seat!", "hands!". It took a moment for George to untangle his face from the distortion that disgust had made it before he yelled back to us: "no, no, no-its your brain! Your mind is the most important aid you have!" Ahhh, yes, of course!

I think no one would dispute that riding is a 'thinking' activity. Unlike sports like weight lifting, or shot put, where the act is one of sheer power and force, riding is about strategy. You have to delicately balance the demands of the course, your horse and yourself. Often, however, we may lose sight of just how important a tool our brains are, and become entrenched in self-defeating patterns. But exactly why should you be reading a book such as this one, or considering developing mental skills?

Well, most of you obviously know the importance of physical training. Everyday you go out and practice, develop skills and set goals. The very word training implies there is some sort of preparation that is specific and focused. Not one of you will debate the fact that you need to physically train you and your horse in order to be better at your sport. You also know that practice, commitment, and desire are essential to this undertaking.

But what about how you use your body from the neck up? Is it desirable to attain a greater level of emotional control, to learn to cope with competitive pressures, to problem solve effectively? And if this is important to your riding goals, then do these tasks not take a certain amount of commitment and practice as well? Shouldn't you put effort into training mentally the way you train physically? If you would like to become a complete rider, and have a considerable edge in competitive situations, the answer has to be yes.

So why don't more riders put the time and effort needed into the psychological aspects of their training? I think its because the field of sport psychology or the idea of mental training has become confused with 'psyching up' or being motivated enough, and of course most riders think they have enough motivation. So this definition is far too simplistic-its kind of like saying all there is to being a superior rider is repeating 'I think I can, I think I can' over and over. So why should you look at the psychological aspect of your training more closely? I'll give you three solid reasons to consider:

You are what you think:

This can be a blessing or a curse, depending on the nature and quality of your thinking. You can start by asking yourself: what is your vision of yourself right now? Is it one of being strong and competent? Is it possible to see yourself winning at this time? Or when you conjure up an image of yourself competing do you see yourself falling apart, choking? This is an incredible indication of where you are right now -because it really is true: you cannot do it until you see it happen in your mind. Many, many people deep down believe that they don't deserve to win, and they won't, until that belief is changed.

Mental strength is a tie breaker:

You can be the best physically on that particular day and still not win because you were not mentally prepared. Psychological readiness is what sets athletes apart. Consider the Olympics, all the best in the world are there, and all physically well prepared. What then separates the truly superior athletes is mental fitness. Consider Ian Miller, some believe that his mental abilities come naturally to him and that may be true. What is indisputable is his ability to focus, which was reportedly in the 99th percentile when he was tested by a sport psychologist not long ago. Ian's skills are attainable to others, however, they can be learned through education and practice.

You are already doing it:

Mental training is something you are already engaged in everyday, either you do it ineffectively or you do it effectively. Think about it, everyday you are "training yourself" - you are giving yourself certain messages about the kind of athlete you are or about how to interpret that nervous feeling in your stomach. Some people choose to utilize this information and some do not. Those who do make a choice to be aware of what is happening 'from the neck up' are mindful of the messages they are giving themselves and the emotional reactions they are experiencing. A good analogy to think of is the training of your horse. Everyday you teach your horse something. It may be you are teaching him to move off your left leg better, or because you are unaware of proper technique, or unaware in general, you could be teaching him to be unresponsive to your left leg. It is the same with your mental training, if you don't get educated and aware, you may be ingraining harmful or counterproductive messages into your head. What's more, you'll have no idea why things go right when they do and therefore make it more difficult for yourself to replicate that performance state again.

***Mental training is something you are engaged in every day,
you either do it ineffectively or effectively***

These are the beliefs I have formulated from being a competitive rider for 15 years. When I was starting out I, like many of you, was not blessed with the most expensive or most talented of mounts. Today I am thankful for that experience. It caused me to look in a different direction. If I could not do anything about the physical limitations of my horse, then what did I have control over? The answer was me. My mind. I had control over that, and once I realized this things began to change. In fact I can even remember the specific day that happened and how my riding came to evolve after that. I decided that looking at this aspect of my riding was going to be my competitive edge. What this focus did for me is it made me a very consistent competitor. When others were cracking under the pressure of a big class, I stayed cool. My first reward for my perseverance was a junior hunter championship at an A show. I won this championship without ever winning a class all week at the show. Why? I was more consistent than anyone else and that led to more points. So my fate might have been to be stuck in thinking about how my horse didn't measure up, and get discouraged when I rode well and did not win. I have no doubt that would have led me to lose more and more confidence. Focusing on improving my riding in a means that was directly under my control did improve my riding, gave me confidence and the winning, although it came in a slightly different form, took care of itself.

As you read this book, if I could leave you with something to think about in terms of your own training it would be this: you know that in order to develop physically as an athlete you need to first become aware of your physical abilities. In other words, to make corrections and improve physically you first have to have an awareness of the mistakes you are making. The same principle applies to mental training-in order to begin to develop psychologically as an athlete,

11

you first must develop an awareness of your psychological state. So make a commitment to begin to develop that awareness, to become mindful, and that can be your first step in utilizing the other half of your resources (those from the neck up) to achieve your riding goals.

Discipline is a key ingredient in success

Change begins with an awareness of where you are now

Tips for using this manual:

- Refer the Appendix, where you will find a quick mental skills assessment. You can use these questions as a 'before and after' guide for how your psychological skills are progressing.

- Practice developing one skill at a time, do not overwhelm yourself.

- Make your trainer aware of what you are trying to accomplish so they can support you in your goals.

- Consider how these skills can be useful in other areas of your life.

- Use the space provided for you to write down your thoughts and notes, or invest in a journal.

Part One

LEARNING
THE BASICS

Chapter
1

Where are you Going?

Wherever you go, there you are.....
-source unknown

We all know that you have to have some idea of where it is you are going before you can get there. The concept is simple, but many people do not consider its relevance to everyday life and to sport. After all, you wouldn't start out driving one day without knowing where you where headed to, and if you didn't consider your destination, of course you wouldn't get there. Knowing your destination is another way of thinking about goal setting.

To succeed...You need to find something to hold on to, something to
motivate you, something to inspire you.
—Tony Dorsett

Discovering your Motivation

Monica was feeling overwhelmed. Lately her lessons had been going poorly, and today she avoided riding altogether by calling out to the barn and telling her trainer she was sick. Of course this made her feel worse, but she felt she just didn't want to face it today. The truth is, Monica doesn't like the idea of competing at major shows, and feels she is being pushed beyond her ability each time she has a lesson. Her trainer believes, as she has not heard different, that Monica wants to go all the way to the top with her riding. She cannot understand, however, the lack of interest Monica has displayed in this goal and is getting frustrated with her not trying. The truth is, Monica is not being true to her original aspirations (to have fun and to have a hobby) but she is unaware this has happened and therefore is unable to articulate it to anyone else.

If you don't enjoy the training and competition aspects of your riding, you may lose your motivation and will to participate. You may begin to feel discouraged, helpless and lose your confidence. This statement seems remarkably simple, but it is also very true. Research has strongly shown that athletes who lose their sense of pleasure also lose their interest and motivation.

Many riders suffer problems with commitment to their sport. This is not because they have lost interest in riding or competing, but is usually due to the fact that they have lost sight of why they are riding. Knowing what your motivation is possibly the most important piece of information you can possess. It will mean the difference between whether you feel confident, content and be able to look forward to riding. And yes, you should.

Stop for a minute and think about what you wished to achieve when you began your sport. What is it that intrigued you about it? Why did you choose your specific sport and what did you hope to accomplish? What is the meaning behind why you ride?

Take a moment to write down your reflections:

_____

_____

_____

_____

_____

_____

_____

_____

Now write a "guiding statement" that reflects the motivation behind your commitment:

Examples: "I ride because I love the pleasure of learning"
               "I ride because I love to train horses"
               "I ride to win"

Your Guiding Statement:

_____

_____

This statement is your fuel. It will help propel you to reach your goals. There will be times when you lose hope and feel frustrated. If you think about your guiding statement, or why you ride, it can help you slog through the tough stuff. Consider all those brave individuals who have battled Mount Everest.

Some undertook the challenge in order to stand "on top of the world", others wanted the ultimate physical challenge, some were retracing the steps of people who had walked that path before. For others still, it was a spiritual quest. Whatever the motivation, this knowledge helped them to endure incredible physical and psychological pain. The tough stuff was made bearable because at the end of it all, there was a why. So find your why, and keep it close to you. You'll find it can whisper encouragement, and prop you up when you don't feel like going on anymore.

"A man who knows why can deal with almost any how"
-Victor Frankl

Be HONEST about your motivation, it will help you to set your goals more effectively

Pleasure=Commitment=Success

Dream A Little Dream

Before beginning to lay out your plan of attack, define your dream without censoring yourself. Do you dream of riding in the Olympics? Winning a championship or grand prix? Becoming a world class instructor? Then ask yourself, what would I be doing just before I reached my dream? Then just before that, and so on.....This will give you a rough road map of where you are traveling.....

completing your dream tree:

your dream

_____

_____

what would you be doing just before
your dream happened

_____

_____

_____

and just before this?

_____

_____

_____

and just before this?

_____

_____

and just before this?

_____

_____

and just before this?

_____

_____

_____

As you travel down the dream tree, you will notice a few things about your answers. The statements at the top reflect your long term goals, and the statements toward the bottom, your short term. Your statements should become more and more specific - if you took it to the extreme, at the bottom you would find the goal of getting on a horse! Every dream, no matter how large or ambitious, can be broken down into simple steps. For this reason, you may also notice that as you get toward the bottom of your tree, the goals seem to be more achievable. Allow this to give you confidence that you can achieve what you want, if you break it down into attainable action.

Allow yourself to dream before you set your goals

Commitment and Priorities

Once you have reviewed your motivation and dreams, the next set of questions you may want to consider are:

1.   What are other priorities in your life, school, partner, kids, job etc.

_____

_____

_____

2.   Where does the priority of your sport rank?

_____

_____

_____

3.   How does your time and energy reflect or not reflect these priorities?

_____

_____

_____

4.   How do your goals currently reflect these priorities?

_____

_____

_____

Commitments should reflect priority and priority should reflect how much time and energy you devote to your sport goals

A lower priority in your life does not mean you have to be less of a rider. It may mean that you take a longer time to develop skills, it may mean that your not going to the Olympics, it may mean that your goals are stretched out over a longer period of time. It is important that you are truthful with yourself about your motivation and commitment. If what you want out of your sport is fun and learning, then your approach will be different from someone who wants to reach the top. This has nothing to do with one person being better or more committed than the other, it means their priorities are different and the way in which they construct their training and expectations will be different.

You have to expect things of yourself before you can do them.
—Michael Jordan

Understand what skills you will need

Here is an important step not to be missed. Now that you have uncovered your motivation, done a little uncensored dreaming, and considered your commitment, you need to undertake a skills inventory. What physical and mental skills do you ultimately need to reach your dream? You can begin to collect data on this question by asking your trainer. Next, you can study and interview people who are already doing what you want to do. How did they get there? What did they have to learn? How close are you to possessing these skills?

_____

_____

_____

Mapping out a plan of action

A lot of people think (and rightly so) that setting goals is easy, its reaching them that's the hard part. Knowing how to set goals that will be effective for you is difficult, and involves a lot of careful thought. To begin with, goal setting is a highly individualized process. Athletes differ with respect to both types of goals and strategies. Two athletes involved in the same sport may have very different looking goals and very different ideas in how they may achieve them. By now, you have some idea why you want to ride, and what your dreams are. Now you need a plan, which means, oh yes, work! Action!

Even if you are on the right track, you'll get run over if you just sit there.
—Will Rogers

Will Rogers was one smart man. Having identified your track, you cannot afford to just stand (or sit!) there. You have to get moving, so lets begin.....

Define a goal that you would like to achieve for yourself. You can choose a goal from the bottom end of your 'dream tree'.	**Advancing to the next level of competition**
Decide whether the goal is one which will be achieved in the near future (short term), or is it a goal which will be reached after some time (long term)	**Long term**
Consider to what degree you will have control over the achievement of your goal. (self-controlled = is within your power to achieve, combination controlled = there are things you can do to achieve this goal but a certain amount of it is based on factors over which you have little control, external control = you probably have almost no control over the factors which may help you achieve this goal).	**Mostly within my control, although I have to consider the readiness and ability of my horse as well. However, my trainer has assured me he can manage the bigger jumps.**

Develop a step by step strategy that outlines how you're going to get there. It may help to visualize yourself attaining the goal, and then begin to ask yourself questions like, "What would I be doing right before that happened?"

1. Be able to do an entire course at the same height the fences in this new division will be in the show ring.
2. Develop confidence over bigger fences, and to do this I need to..
3. Gradually introduce myself and my horse to bigger jumps. I can speak to my trainer about how we may begin to do this.
4. Work on my body position, which in my case means having the physical strength to hold my body over fences.
5. Become more consistent with my timing or 'eye' for a fence.

Consider what barriers may get in the way of you attaining your goal. Time constraints? Physical injury? Money? Make sure you incorporate strategies to overcome these barriers.

My nerves will likely be my biggest obstacle. I will need to draw up another plan to practice controlling my emotions.

Make sure you leave room to evaluate and reevaluate your goals. Writing your goals down in a sport journal or diary can ensure you are keeping track of your strategies and progress. You want to be able to reflect on and assess how the strategy worked; was it less realistic than you first thought? Too ambitious? Perhaps you will need to select an alternate plan.

In writing down her thoughts in a journal and tracking her progress, this rider realized that she had been correct in assessing this goal to be longer term. She found she had to take each of her steps, and break them down into smaller detail. This left her with a number of shorter terms goals which were manageable, and she found this helped her confidence considerably.

As you can see from the above example, the process of writing out your goals will help you to get clear on what specific steps are needed. Instead of gambling that things will work out, you are defining a specific plan, or creating a map of how to arrive at your chosen destination. It is also important to realize that your goals will incorporate the physical and the psychological. The rider in the example above realized her nerves may be a barrier to her achieving her goal. The mind and the body do work together. The more you guide yourself to think in these terms, (that is why I wrote this book!) the more successful your training efforts will be.

One important note on the concept of writing down your goals. There is no 'magic' per se in this, what happens is it tends to simply put you into a frame of mind that says 'what can I now do to get there ?' It then stands to reason that the more that you think along these lines, the more likely you will be to achieve your goals (of course!).

> ***If you don't know where you are going,***
> ***any road will get you there..***
> ***-source unknown***

Other tips/suggestions

Create a visual reminder of your goal:
One year the Saskatchewan Roughriders were all seen wearing tape around their ring fingers in training - as a reminder of where they would be wearing their grey cup rings. Well, they did end up wearing those rings! I have no doubt that the effect of seeing that reminder day after day was this: they were constantly thinking 'what can I do to get there'. So go ahead and tape that picture of Ian Millar up on the lid of your tack box, save a place on the wall for that championship, put other pictures or reminders on your fridge of your dream.

Tell somebody about your goals:
Letting your trainer know about your goals and reviewing them on occasion is vital. This person is a very integral member of your 'team'. He/she is going to

guide you with respect to developing the physical skills you will need to succeed. Doing this can also mean avoiding painful misunderstandings, as in the example of Monica given at the beginning of this chapter. Besides your coach, you may want to consider sharing your goals with others as well. When you tell somebody about your plans, and talk about them often, it has the effect of igniting your commitment. It may also open the door for you to receive support and encouragement from those closest to you.

State your goals positively:

Here is a little gem that I try to live by:

Moving toward success is not the same thing as avoiding failure

This is very important! Pause for a moment, close your eyes and try to visualize what this statement means. When we are in a mind-set of moving toward success, we are consciously considering what we need to do to get there. Conversely, when we are in a mind-set of avoiding failure, we are expending all of our energy trying to figure out ways to avoid pain and disappointment. This leaves little energy and resources for anything else.

Consider the rider that is afraid of failing. This fear becomes a guiding statement that rules her choices and behavior. While riding into the ring her thoughts are focused on nothing but 'don'ts'. "Don't forget to get the right pace, don't forget to keep my reins short, don't let my horse drop his shoulder in the corners". Before long her anxiety is rising, the first mistake happens and guess what? This rider will be stuck in this mistake for some time.

So, when you are setting or stating your goals, make sure you are stating them positively, or in terms of what you will do. For example, "I will not fall off this week" is negatively stated. "I will work on feeling more confident in my position this week" is the same goal, stated positively. Avoid "don'ts", "nevers" and "will nots" in your goals statements.

Make sure your goals are challenging enough:

Some riders do make the mistake of setting goals that are too easy. In order to grow, and reap the benefits of self esteem and confidence, you need to have goals that lead you to extend yourself. Taking some time to have a discussion with your trainer about what may be an appropriate, yet challenging goal may be helpful.

Know how you will measure your goals

Let's say that your goal is to improve the quality of your equitation. What you need to ask yourself is, what will be different about my riding when I reach this goal? Will I be able to hold my leg position more consistently over fences? Will my back be straighter? Will my seat be more secure? If your goal is getting to the airport, you will know you are getting closer when you see that sign "airport, 5km". Consider what 'signs' you need to be watching for that will tell you that you have made progress.

Consider setting a time frame for your goal:

The act of setting a deadline for your goal forces you to evaluate your progress, and if necessary, redefine your goal or develop different strategies to meet that goal. Knowing you have a deadline also helps keep you 'accountable'.

Some reasons why people fail to meet their goals

Your goals are not realistic:

Your goals should accurately reflect your current skill level, and your time available to meet the demands of the goal. That is why the inventory you did at the beginning of this chapter with respect to your commitment level is so important. Another important point to remember is to take care to make sure that you are not setting too many goals, or you may become overwhelmed and feel like giving up.

You are setting goals that are too general or vague:

Your goals should be clear and specific. "I want to be more effective when riding in jump-offs" is a great goal, but this statement says nothing about what you will do to get there. What skills do you need? Always break down your goals to their simplest form.

Because you set goals and then fail to evaluate and reevaluate:
Many riders develop strategies and then are unwilling to abandon them, even if its perfectly clear that they are not working. And you may be interested to know that there is a name for this phenomenon-its called "mindlessness"! If you try and try, and keep getting that 'error message' its likely time to admit defeat. So evaluate! And please, if its not working, try something different!

Your goals are all focused on outcomes, instead of process:
If you tend to focus solely on outcome, chances are you'll be setting yourself up for more failures and feelings of disappointment. **Outcome-related goals** are assessed in black and white terms, or winning and losing. Take heed of what John Candy playing a coach in the movie Cool Runnings said to one of his bobsledders: "if it's all about winning, then you have to keep on winning." Another flaw of outcomes goals is that they do not afford you as much control over feeling successful. Factors such as bad judging, poor weather or a less talented mount are out of your control and can impede your chances of winning.

By contrast, with **process goals** the focus is one of improving skills or looking at what you need (what process) to get to a higher level of performance. So even if you did not win the class because your horse tripped in the corner, you will still feel successful if your goal was to keep your pace and get all your distances. You can see how this type of goal also tends to promote constructive analysis of your performance. The main point here to keep in mind is: how you set your goals will determine how you perceive yourself as a rider. Obviously, process goals are more effective both in terms of increasing skill level and maintaining a positive outlook.

Outcome goal:

"I want to win a class at the next competition"

Process goal:

"My goal at this competition is to take more risks in the jump-offs, I want to see if I can take some time off my round by utilizing the skills I have been practicing."

***How you set your goals will ultimately determine
how you see yourself as a rider***

In short, it is important to look at what your definition of success is. Try not to make it too difficult for yourself to succeed, make it challenging but possible. Strive to formulate a definition of success that is broad enough to include many opportunities for feeling good about your riding.. Take a moment to ask yourself what your current definitions of success and failure are all about and write down your reflections:

Success to me means:

_____

_____

_____

_____

Failure to me means:

_____

_____

_____

_____

So again, (this point is well worth repeating!) if success is all about winning classes, (getting that red ribbon in hand) then the percentage of time in which you do feel successful is going to be small. That means your confidence will suffer and you may actually end up winning less of those red ribbons. This is why a lot of people shy away from goal setting- because they are afraid they will not be able to measure up to those standards when all is said and done. You all know this I'm sure from past attempts at setting new years resolutions. It's the mind set of: 'if I don't set any goals, nobody gets hurt.'

Remember: motivation is your fuel, goals are your
direction (your map) to your ultimate
destination (your dreams)

Key Points:

- Always keep in mind why riding is important to you.

- Don't forget to dream - uncensored!

- Decide on what commitment level works for you, considering other priorities in your life.

- Clearly define your map (plan of action).

- From time to time, reevaluate your goals.

Chapter
2

Talking the Talk...

***How you talk to yourself has a
big impact on your performance***

'Don't think about purple cows'

How many of you were able to resist thinking about a brightly colored bovine? I'm willing to bet not a single one of you. That is because words are very powerful, and because the brain does not process 'don't' very well. This example serves to illustrate just how powerful our own thoughts or 'self-talk' can be. Think about it, every time you talk to yourself inside your head (which is often!) you are giving yourself directions and suggestions about what to focus on and how to behave.

***Change your thoughts and you change your world
-Norman Vincent Peale***

How you talk to yourself=
what you believe about yourself

How riders 'talk to themselves', not surprisingly, is directly related to their confidence level. We all spend vast amounts of time talking to ourselves, and much of the time we are not even aware of what we are saying to ourselves. Nevertheless, these thoughts effect our feelings which in turn effect our actions. Confident riders monitor the content and frequency of their thoughts. They know how to shut off negative internal dialogue and replace it with positive statements. In effect, they have been able to 'train' themselves to think in certain ways that encourage success. This is not to simply say that they repeat "I think I can" over and over ad nauseam. Good self talk involves thinking constructively, positively and realistically. Unfortunately, our minds are not always on our side, and we do have to consciously, through effort and awareness, 'train' ourselves to think differently.

Awareness

The first task you have to consider in realigning your self talk is to make yourself aware of how much, and what you are saying. I recall hearing about a golf instructor who gave his student 100 paper clips to carry while playing, and every time she thought negatively she was to shift one paper clip from her front pocket to her back pocket. To her horror, she ended up with 87 paper clips in her back pocket! You can use a method similar to this one, or try keeping a sport journal, where you write down your thoughts after a ride. Be patient with increasing your awareness, it will take time to get yourself used to 'thinking about your thinking'.

It has been my experience that the most effective method of promoting awareness about your thoughts is to write them down. When you do this, you are forced to bring into consciousness what you are thinking. Negative thoughts by their nature tend to be insidious, and creep by without our knowing. Try this experiment: spend one week recording the content of your thoughts. You may want to focus in on a specific area such as self talk in lessons, how you talk to yourself while you are preparing to ride, or when you are working out a specific problem:

Situation

Automatic Thoughts

examples:

Missing a distance in a lesson

"I never get it right"
"I am such a loser"

Tacking up before a ride

"I hope I don't fall off today"
"I feel down today, I probably won't ride well"

_____

_____

_____

_____

_____

_____

_____

_____

A man is not hurt so much by what happens,
as by his opinion of what happens
-Michel Eyquem De Montaigne

A word about perception

What is it that causes you to begin thinking such negative and destructive thoughts in the first place? Some may say that the thoughts they have are inevitable, given the situations they find themselves in. If my horse spooks and ruins my chance at a ribbon, how can I not think it was stupid of me not to lunge him before my class? The fact is, it is not negative events that cause negative thinking to occur. Rather, it is our perception of the event which will determine the content of our thoughts, which interact with our feelings, and then, produce our actions.

Event → *thoughts* → ← *feelings* → *action or behaviour*

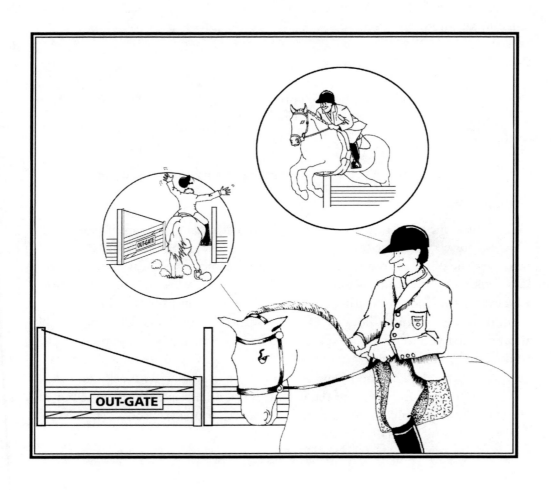

Your 'self-talk' reflects your expectations

For example, both Rider A and Rider B have missed the distance to their first fence in an important class.

Rider A thinks:

> "I've screwed up my entire round, I'll never make it up now!"

And Rider B:

> "I have to get more pace going around the next corner"

The event is the same for both, yet the emotional and mental response is different for each. Rider A perceives the event to mean failure, Rider B perceives the event to mean the need to change something about their strategy. Lets look at another, "non-riding" example, suppose I asked you to walk across a board on the floor, measuring 1 foot wide. You would probably do so without thinking much about it. If I now suspended that board 100 feet in the air and asked you to do the same, you would immediately become more anxious not because the task had changed, but because your perception of the task had changed. The good news is that actively changing your self talk can help to alter your perception of the event. A stake class can become just the same as a course you completed during the week, or one you rode at home during a lesson if you talk to yourself the right way.

> ***Our life is what our thoughts make it***
> ***-Marcus Aurelius***

Identifying the Problem

Now that you have increased your awareness as to what you are thinking, and you understand how your thoughts and feelings interact to produce action, you want to move on to looking at what is distorted, counterproductive, or negative about your thinking patterns. The following are the most common problem areas, adapted from Dr. David Burns' *The Feeling Good Handbook*.

"Should/Must/Always/Never" Thinking:
This distortion leads you to criticise yourself and sometimes others will "shoulds", "musts", "always" and "nevers".

Examples: "I should place in every class", "I always miss my distance to oxers", "I never get anything right"

Negative Labelling:
When you negatively label yourself, you identify yourself with a negative trait or shortcoming. In other words, you tell yourself you are the negative trait or behaviour.

Examples: "I am a loser", "I am a jerk", "I am weak"

Here are some more examples of negative labels, check any you tend to use:

demanding	stupid	wimpy
dumb	overly sensitive	unimportant
emotional	passive	hysterical
incapable	lazy	rigid
bossy	illogical	non-competitive

A special note here, sometimes these words do describe aspects of our behaviour that we would like to change. For example, maybe you would like to strive to be less sensitive because you find yourself overreacting to criticism. This is a fair goal, as you are trying to modify your behaviour so you can learn more effectively.

Catastrophizing:
"Catastrophizing' involves turning small flaws or negative experiences into major earth shattering problems.

Example: "I can't stand this, this always happens to me"

Personalizing:
When you personalize events, you blame yourself for events that were not entirely your responsibility, or you may blame others and overlook ways that your own behaviour contributed to the problem.

Example: "If it weren't for the poor ring conditions, I would have won that class"

Mind Reading/Fortune Telling:
These two types of distorted thinking involve making assumptions about people or events without enough information.

Examples: "I know I won't be able to make that turn", "I know he's trying to psych me out"

Emotional reasoning:
This form of negative thinking involves reasoning from how you feel.

Example: "I feel like a loser, so I must be one"

Don't thinking:
Look again at the example about the purple cows. Purple cows will always win, and that's because, as stated earlier, our mind has a hard time interpreting 'don't'. Think about it. What does "don't round your shoulders" or "don't look down" look like? It is very difficult for our brains to formulate a picture of 'don't'. What usually happens instead is that it takes the latter part of the message - "round your shoulders" and "look down" and focuses on this and brings it into reality. In other words, you end up rounding your shoulders and looking down, or the very action you were trying to avoid has come true.

Black and white thinking:
When you think this way, everything is all or nothing . You either succeed or fail, you are either right or wrong. This type of thinking is typical of people who are perfectionists. There is also a strong relationship between this kind of thinking and anxiety and depression.

Example: "I missed my lead in that class so it was a disaster" or "I messed up completely because my horse spooked in the corner"

Positive filter:
This type of thinking means that you 'filter out' anything positive, and dwell on all that is negative.

Example: "I had a terrible show" (even though you placed in several classes)

As a next step, take the thoughts you have recorded, or start a new form, and try identifying how your thoughts are distorted or unreasonable:

Situation	Automatic Thoughts	Distortion
Your horse stops filter	"I always blow it!"	catastrophizing, positive
You miss a lead	"I never get my leads"	black and white thinking
A fellow rider comments on your riding	"I know that person was trying to psych me out"	mind reading
You fall off	"I'm such a lousy rider!"	labelling

_____

_____

_____

_____

_____

_____

_____

_____

_____

Changing the content of your thoughts

Your next step in managing our self talk is learning to change negative thoughts. As we have seen, most negative thoughts are 'distorted' in some way, that is, they are not accurate and our perception is faulty. Your 'replacement' thoughts should be positive, constructive and realistic.

Stop the pattern of negative thinking

Sometimes it is helpful to put an abrupt halt to the negative pattern we are in before we seek to change our thoughts. This is especially true when your thoughts are spinning out of control and everything seems negative and you feel overwhelmed. There are a few ways you may seek to accomplish this. One is to use the skill of *centering*. When you use this technique, you shift your focus from your thoughts to your breathing, thereby giving you a 'break' from the negative pattern. Another way is to *visualize* a big red stop sign and shout to yourself (inside your head!) "STOP!" You could also choose another image that is meaningful to you, such as imaging a big red "X" through your thoughts, or erasing a blackboard with all your negative thinking on it. Yet another technique is to put a *visual image to your 'critic'*, such as the devil, or a cranky ornery old toad (whatever your imagination can conceive!), then you push them out or throw them out of the way. You can have a lot of fun and be creative with this technique, and it works especially well for young children.

Challenge the evidence

One way of challenging negative thoughts is to gather evidence to refute them. The problem with some negative thinking is that it encourages your mind to start searching for evidence to support those statements, and guess what, it can usually easily find them. For example, you may have missed getting your leads in a class a total of 6 times out of 100+ times in one show, but if you make the statement "I never get my leads", you will think of those six times, begin to magnify them, and then what? How will you feel? Pretty bad! And what's more, you will have placed yourself in a position where you are unlikely to search for any solution. Negative thinking does not beget problem solving.

Try this exercise: pretend you are a lawyer and you are being asked to refute a belief (your negative self statement) by gathering and presenting all the evidence to the contrary (ie.: what exactly is the probability that you will fall off again, given the facts of the situation?). This approach is effective in terms of getting you logically, as opposed to emotionally oriented. In other words, it automatically forces you into a problem-solving state of mind.

Reframe your thoughts

It is always possible, as we discussed earlier, to see the same situation more than one way. In our discussion of butterflies earlier in the book we talked about how physical changes in the body could either be labelled as anxiety or intensity, depending on our view. When you notice your heart beating faster, tell may tell yourself: "I must be really nervous" or you may tell yourself: "I am getting ready to compete, this is a good sign!" Or, when you are faced with a tough competitor, you could respond with "I can never win against this person", or "I am in good company here, we both made it to this level so we both must have what it takes to win". When you attempt to reframe your thoughts, you ask yourself: "is there another way I can see this?"

With these ideas in mind, now try taking those thoughts you identified earlier, challenge them, and identify more appropriate thoughts for each situation:

Automatic Thoughts	Distortion	New Thoughts
"I always blow it!"	catastrophizing, positive filter	"I need to figure out what went wrong, what I need to change for the next time"
"I never get my leads"	black and white 'never' thinking	"I'm working on my leads right now, they are getting better but I will have to accept some mistakes along the way"

_____

_____

_____

_____

_____

_____

_____

_____

_____

Here is another example of the process you need to follow in replacing your negative thoughts:

1.   Identify your automatic thought(s)

      "I always screw up"

2.   Identify the type of distortion(s) present in your thought(s). In this example:

      black and white thinking, exaggeration, positive filter

3.   Challenge the negative thought by asking yourself questions like: what evidence do I have that this will happen? Even if it has happened in the past, how many times? (Challenge that 'always' or 'never')

      "I have had lots of successes, in other words,
      * I don't 'always screw up'"*

4.   Identify a more appropriate belief. Make sure it is stated positively and specifically, don't just say 'I will never think that again'. State your preferred response in terms of what you will do.

      "I made a mistake, and now I need to analyse why that happened
      and make a plan to correct the problem. I have to expect I will
      make some mistakes along the way, and that's how I will learn to
      be better."

Three Rules to remember in changing your self talk:

1.   *Realistic:* Your 'replacement thoughts' should reflect more appropriate (realistic) beliefs.

2.   *Positive:* Make sure your thoughts are stated positively and specifically, don't just say 'I will never think that again'. State your preferred response in terms of what you will do. This is lesson number two in self-talk: state what you want to do/or see happen in positive terms. For instance, "I will keep my back straight", and "I will keep my eyes on the line in front of me".

3.   *Constructive:* Have your thoughts lead to an action, or promote problem solving.

Remember that every time you are thinking you are in essence talking to yourself. Given that we think almost constantly about something throughout the day, that's a lot of 'self-talk'. It makes sense then, to learn to pay attention to, and control its content for your benefit.

Uses for self talk

In addition to seeking to change the quality of your thoughts to make them more positive and constructive, you also can and should use self talk in a pro-active manner. For example:

Learning new skills - When you are in the early learning phase, talking to yourself and giving yourself certain cues can be extremely effective. For example, if you are learning to ask for a lead change you may repeat to **yourself** as you prepare to ask yourself: "right leg behind the girth, left leg at the girth, outside rein steady".

Building confidence - When your self talk mirrors your positive beliefs in yourself, and your goals, you boost your confidence. Affirmations are an effective way of promoting positive beliefs about yourself. An affirmation is very simply a short, positive statement that describes a state you would like to encourage in yourself. For example:

"I am a strong and confident rider"

"I am calm and confident"

"I make sure that I take not only the time to work at achievement, but also the time to enjoy the pleasure of riding along the way"

"I allow no one to impose the pressures of their demands on me without my choice, my acceptance, and my approval."

"I am focused and alert"

"I have the courage to do what I need to do to get where I want to go"

At this point, you may want to look back on the first chapter and consider what goals you developed for yourself, and then write an affirmation to reflect each one of these goals. You can think of these as "prayers" in the way that when you repeat them to yourself, you are honouring your ability and your dreams.

As cues to focus, relax or energize - You can choose 'key words' that reflect what you want to accomplish. Below are some examples, but you can use anything that holds meaning for you.

To relax	To focus your attention	To energize
calm	be here	go
slow	now	psych
easy	center	intense
wait	focus	forward
quiet	look	fire

Your self talk does mirror your beliefs,
and behaviour - for better or worse

Key Points:

• Awareness is key. Develop an understanding of how you talk to yourself.

• Learn to be able to detect when yourself talk gets off track

• Actively replace your negative thoughts with positive, realistic and constructive thoughts.

• Be patient, it will take a while to form the habit of thinking about your thinking.

Chapter
3

The Movies you Play

How visualization can help you to perform better

***The mind is the limit. As long as the mind can envision the fact
that you can do something, you can do it—as long
as you really believe 100 percent.***
—Arnold Schwarzenegger

What is visualization or imagery?

Imagery is very simply a mental picture created by our imaginations. Often we
use imagery without even being aware of it. For example, if you are afraid of
performing in front of other people, not only are you telling yourself negative
things which are provoking your anxiety, but chances are you are also seeing
negative images. You may imagine people whispering behind your back or

snickering at your expense. It is also likely that while you are running such pictures through your mind that you begin to feel not only the anxiety associated with such a scene, but actual physiological reactions like perspiration, shaking and dry mouth. In this way, the images we create in our minds are very powerful. To our minds, they are no different than reality. To explain this phenomenon further, think about a bad dream you have had, did you know you were dreaming? Did you wake up full of anxiety and perhaps shaking? Most of us do experience such reactions to images that we created ourselves while sleeping, that clearly were not real. Images we form in a waking state may be just as powerful.

You cannot do it until you see it happen in your mind

The skills you need

There are a wide range of individual differences with respect to people's capacities to form images. We all have the ability to do so, however may do so very differently or may experience blocks from time to time. Imagery skill, however, does respond very well to practice. A simple way to do so is to imagine something with which you are very familiar, such as your home. Or, you may want to place an object in front of you, study it carefully, and then close your eyes and try and recreate it in your imagination. In addition, some people experience imagery by touching or kinesthetic means, by hearing, (auditory) or smell (olfactory). All of these senses can be thought of as imagery, and of course the more senses through which you experience what you are imagining, the more realistic it will seem. If you can only use one sense, or your pictures are in black and white instead of color, don't panic. It is important that you go with your strength while also trying to further develop your imagery skills.

There are two perspectives from which you may use to visualize. The first is seeing yourself as if you are watching yourself on video. Here you see yourself from a distance, close up, or whatever inventive camera angle you choose, performing. The second is to see and feel yourself as if you were in your own body. This is the most effective form of visualization as it allows you to bring in your sense of feel. Most people find it easier to see themselves outside of themselves, however, visualizing from within is a skill you should seek to develop if you want the best results. The following are some examples of visualization exercises on horseback which encourage the development of the skill of 'inner body' imagery:

Exercise:

A)   Action: Sit on your horse, take up your reins, and back your horse up a few steps. Do this a few times, taking note of what you see and feel while you are performing the action. For example, what muscles are you using and what does the tension feel like?

Visualize: Return to your start position, and this time close your eyes and perform the same action in your mind, seeing and feeling yourself doing it.

B)   Action: Start at one corner of the ring and trot to the next corner, again concentrating on what you see and how you feel while you are doing it. Are you focusing your eyes down the ring, on your hands? What do you see in front of you? What do you notice about how your muscles feel, how your horse feels?

Visualize: Return to your start position, close your eyes and attempt to form a clear and vivid image of you doing this same action. Remember to see and feel.

You can practice imagery easily on a daily basis while you are riding or in your lessons. Simply stop every once in a while and attempt to see and feel what you just did on your horse. If you are in a group lesson situation, take advantage of the time you have while waiting for your turn. Experiment with visualizing that line you are about to ride or the half pass you are working on. Practice and keep track of your progress.

Visualizing in real time, slow motion and fast motion

You can visualize at different 'speeds' as well. When you visualize in slow motion, you see and feel yourself slowly performing a skill or entire course. Slow motion visualization is particularly useful when you are learning a new skill, because you can slow down and isolate elements of the skill so you can see and feel them clearly. Fast motion visualization doesn't necessarily mean that you are visualizing at the speed of light. Rather, that you are seeing your movie at a speed which is a little faster than it would actually take you to perform in real life. This is probably the most commonly used speed. Real time imagery is just what it suggests, performing in your mind in the same time it takes to actually perform what you are visualizing. It allows you to really focus on the whole performance, experiencing each and every component.

What visualization can do for your performance

With practice, imagery can help you to practice skills, deal with anxiety, cope with specific problems and achieve peak performance. Some may think of imagery as 'just an exercise', but this is far too simple a description. Imagery reinforces the memory responses that you will need when you engage in riding - it also sets up the proper physical responses for your muscles to follow - in short it helps to "groove" the correct performance. Studies have repeatedly shown that practicing in your head can be just as effective as actual physical practice. Many athletes use visualization programs because they cannot afford financially to train enough, do not have the proper training facilities, or do not have the time to train enough physically.

Research has shown that imagined events produce the same or close to the same electrical activity in muscles. Sports psychologists who monitored the electrical activity in skiers legs as they imagined skiing an entire course (a real time visualization). They found that the readings of muscular activity changed throughout the imagery, and was greatest when they were skiing rough sections of the course - which would require the greatest muscle activity. So when you imagine an activity, you are using this same neural pathways as you would if you were actually doing the event.

How to Get Started

1.   Keep it simple at first. Don't attempt to visualize the whole performance right away, start with crucial skills or a sequence of event.

2.   Make a decision as to whether you will be attempting to image from your perspective (being 'inside your body') or as a 'member of the audience' (as if you were watching a video of the event). Remember that research on imagery reveals that the 'inside' orientation is the more powerful one.

3.   Decide what it is that is important to focus on. What movements, feelings, critical times in the performance do you need to focus on? Set up a rehearsal goal- for example, is it important for you to become more sensitive to muscle movements, muscle tension or visual cues?

4.   Before you begin your visualization, make sure you are relaxed. Try centering yourself with cycles of deep breathing. Always begin to practice your visualizations in a quiet place, away from distractions. Once you are comfortable with your visualization skills, you can practice on your horse and in noisier places, which is of course what you will have to be able to do when at a horse show.

Everyone possesses the ability to use imagery, but like any other skill, it requires practice and discipline

Using visualization to help you learn

Important!: Before you start imaging, make sure you know what it is you need to do for the proper execution of a skill. If you don't know, check with your coach. If you don't do this, you could inadvertently be training yourself to do the wrong thing over and over! If you know you have done it right before, take some time to write out what the sequence was, and everything else you can recall about it such as how your muscles felt, what your emotions were like etc. so you can recreate the scene for yourself as vividly as possible. If you use some particular cue, like the word 'flow' to remind you to come forward out of the corner to a jump, then incorporate this into your movie as well.

Take some time now to consider a skill you are developing, and ask yourself what is involved in this skill technically, and how it feels when you do it right. Write out your ideas and formulate them into a script you can use for your visualization:

example: riding to a jump from a tight turn

I make sure my horse is in front of my leg and balanced as I approach the turn. I then use my eyes to pick my line. While keeping my eye focused on the jump I gradually shift my weight back and begin to ask for the turn. Then I open my leading rein slightly while balancing with the outside rein and leg and ride forward out of the turn, again keeping my weight and body slightly shifted back.

_____

_____

_____

_____

Using visualization to help you cope

Visualization is very effective in helping you learn to cope with anxieties and fears. Using imagery, you can practice the same anxiety provoking event over and over while learning to relax. This process is referred to as 'desensitization' because you are desensitizing yourself to a fearful situation. 'Systematic desensitization' involves generating a list of least to most fearful situations concerning a particular fear. You then begin with the least fearful situation, and practice until you can visualize the most fearful with little anxiety before moving on to the others on your list. The process is as follows:

1. Center**, then visualize yourself in competition or training just before that moment when you normally become tense.

2. While experiencing the scene, pay attention to the experience of relaxation you had acquired through the centering.

3.   If you discover that you are starting to feel tense, end the scene and return to centering.

4.   When the centering exercise has led you to relax again, switch the scene back on.

5.   When you are capable of visualizing the scene without tension, this signifies that you have now learned how to eliminate the tension.

6.   Repeat without the tension several more times.

**Centering:

1.   Focus your attention on deep breathing, three deep cycles.

2.   Flow the relaxation through each muscle group.

3.   Scan the body to determine if any tension spots remain.

4.   As a final check, continue centered breathing, visualizing each muscle group loosening up (like light bulbs being turned off one by one).

People who become highly anxious often visualize catastrophes (falling off, getting hurt, being ridiculed). If you have this experience, don't panic. Instead, STOP, REWIND, CENTER and then begin your movie again.

Use visualization to help you practice your perfect performance

Special note: the most effective time to use coping imagery is away from the show ring. You do not want to be drawing your awareness and energy toward mistakes or anxiety provoking situations just before you compete. When you are at the competition, it is best to visualize yourself performing flawlessly, or to utilize peak performance imagery.

Peak Performance Imagery

You can use visualization to practice your ideal or perfect performance again and again. Often, it is helpful to develop a 'script' to guide your imagery practice. Think about a time when you felt you performed your personal best. Focus on dissecting the following factors of the performance, an example is given to guide you. Keep in mind your answers will be unique to you and your horse. Strive to draw out as much detail as possible, incorporating as many different senses as you can.

What were you feeling during the warm-up:
During the warm-up I feel a sense of anticipation and excitement. I feel physically secure in the saddle, like my body is strong but relaxed and ready to respond. I am very focused on how my horse feels underneath me, and what I need to do to make him jump confidently.

_____

_____

_____

_____

_____

_____

Directly before the competition:

My mind is focused and calm. I am reviewing the course in my head and taking a deep breath to center myself. I am reminding myself that I have the skills to do what I need to do in the ring. Everything that is required of me I have done before at home.

_____

_____

_____

_____

_____

_____

What was your attitude toward the competition:

I feel confident and eager to compete.

_____

_____

_____

_____

_____

What happens as your round unfolds:

I trot into the ring and stop, taking my last survey of the course. As I pick up the canter I concentrate on getting the pace I will need to maintain. As I begin my round, I notice how effortless it is to ride today. I seem to be completely in harmony with my horse. I can feel his confidence in my directions. Its as if I am in some kind of bubble, where nothing disturbs me from my concentration. I am aware only of reacting to the demands of the course, which I respond to perfectly, communicating with my horse in just the right way. As I finish and make my way toward the outgate, I am aware of the sound of clapping.

_____

_____

_____

_____

_____

Now use this information to write a 'script' of your best performance. Use as much detail as you can, bring your ideal round to life. If you have a videotape of a good performance, you may want to use this to guide you. Once you have developed a script you are comfortable with, you can transfer it to an audio tape to practice with.

MY BEST PERFORMANCE:

_____

_____

_____

_____

_____

_____

_____

_____

_____

_____

_____

Key Points:

- Practice your visualization regularly. You will achieve the best results with a well developed skill.

- Incorporate visualization into your training plans, to assist you in developing new skills even when you can't get to the barn.

- Use peak performance imagery to help you practice seeing and feeling yourself at your best.

Chapter
4

Concentration and Focus

There you are at the in-gate, and your trainer approaches you with the last minute instructions: "just concentrate and you'll be fine". Great, you think to yourself, but just how do I do that-and what am I supposed to be concentrating on? Saying "just concentrate" to someone is a little like saying "just relax" when you're a bundle of nerves-how do you will yourself to do it? Can you?

Unfortunately, you cannot will yourself to concentrate effectively any more than you can command your tense muscles to relax. Concentrating means focusing, not forcing your attention on a particular task while not being distracted by irrelevant information.

Distractions

We can be distracted in two basic ways, either internally by our thoughts and feelings ("I'm so nervous today") or externally by occurrences in the environment (a noisy crowd or an unsportsmanlike opponent). The best of riders become distracted from their performances, the great ones know how to get that focus back again.

What to focus on

The challenge in the sport of riding is that you do have a lot of different cues to attend to: the feel of your horse, your position, the demands of the course. It can very easily become confusing as to what to direct your attention to. Moreover, as human beings, we have a limited capacity of attention, and can only attend to so many things at once. This is somewhat alleviated by the fact that behaviours or skills which are well learned can become 'automatic' and be performed without conscious thought.

When you are first learning a new skill you have to be more analytical or more 'conscious'. You will probably be giving yourself verbal cues as to what you should be focusing on (ie.: "now I'm coming up to this turn, I want to drop my weight to the outside to better balance my horse"). Eventually, these behaviours or skills that you have to think about will become incorporated into your repertoire of automatic behaviours and you will simply react and it will have that 'flow' quality. So if you're a beginner, or are in the process of developing new skills, it will probably be easy for you to become overwhelmed with things to focus on. You may become so busy trying to think that you fail to react to what is happening as you are riding your horse. (I have heard this called, aptly, "paralysis by analysis") What you want to do is choose one element (perhaps your position) to focus on and let the rest go. Then, as it becomes automatic for you to 'keep your heels down' and you won't have to think about that aspect of riding and your attention will be freed up for other things.

Don't succumb to "paralysis by analysis"!

What is 'flow'

The experience of flow is almost like that of meditation. All distractions fade to the background, your performance becomes effortless, and you are bursting with confidence. Some people report feeling as though they are in slow motion, allowing them to savor each perfect aspect of their performance. One of the elements that makes flow possible is having mastered the skills necessary to perform. That is why the professionals can make their performances look effortless-they have a lot of the behaviour or skills locked into their automatic repertoire, and are free to think about things as they happen.

Concentrating means focusing, not forcing your attention on a particular task while not being distracted by irrelevant information.

Different types of attention

There are different types of attention, and often success depends an rider's ability to shift from one to the other. For example, there what is called a 'broad' focus, which is useful in sizing up the demands of a course. A more 'narrow' focus would be needed when approaching a jump. The attentional requirements of riding dictate that there are many times when you will have to be shifting your attention from a broad to narrow focus. For example, when riding a turn you have a broad range of focus so that you can concentrate on the line of fences coming up, but once you have that assessed, you are going to begin to narrow your focus to the jump in front of you.

Different types of attention are often required at different times in your performance

Different Types of Focus	
Broad / External	**Broad / Internal**
Used to rapidly assess a situation (entering and taking in the layout of the entire course)	*Used to analyze and plan (developing a strategy)*
Narrow / External	**Narrow / Internal**
Used to focus exclusively on one or two external cues (the jump in front of you)	*Used to mentally rehearse an upcoming performance or control an emotional state*

Exercises:

To illustrate the difference between a broad and narrow focus, try this exercise:

Relax in a comfortable chair, taking a few deep breaths until your breathing becomes steady, next open your eyes and pick an object across the room and while your doing this, observe as much of the room and everything in it as your field of vision will allow. Now picture a broad funnel into which your mind is moving, at the centre of which is the object you have chosen. Now gradually narrow your focus to include nothing but the object, and then widen it again, gradually, so you can see everything in the room. Think of your mind as a camera lens that can zoom in and out according to your wishes.

To practice shifting your attention from one place to another try:

Choose an object in the room, spend some time studying it carefully, imagine you are a cam era doing a close up on this object. Next, shift your attention to another object in the room, and just as a camera would need to refocus, zero in on the object letting all the other elements of the room fade into the background.

Or you could:

Choose a piece of music that has many instruments in its composition. Alternately choose one instrument and focus in on how it sounds, while letting the others fade out. You can go back and forth between different instruments and practice shifting your attention from one element of the music to another.

Strategies for improving your concentration

Using cues:

Some athletes find it helpful to develop certain cues that can help them to concentrate or to resume their focus should they lose it during competition. A cue can be a single word or string of words that signals to your mind and body that its time to concentrate. For instance, before you go into the ring you may say to yourself: "relax, keep a steady pace, flow from the corners". You may also use cues during a performance, how many depends on your own needs. The important thing is to develop and consistently use a cue which is meaningful to you.

Park your problems:

When you "park" your problems, you make a conscious decision to put a distraction aside, for later consideration if necessary. If you assess what you are focused on to be counterproductive, change the channel back to your original station! That fight you just had with your trainer can wait until later, as can those feelings of tiredness or fatigue.

When I want to consider a particular problem, I open a certain drawer.
When I have settled the matter in my mind, I close that drawer and
open another. When I desire to sleep, I close all the drawers.
-Napoleon

Use a visual image:

You can use visualization to help facilitate the parking process. See yourself putting that worry away into a box, parking it in a space for future consideration, or imagine yourself enclosed in a force field that allows nothing in. Imagine that you are a thick-skinned determined animal such as an elephant or rhinoceros. Experiment with images until you find one that holds meaning for you.

Using relaxation:

When you are out of focus, and things are whipping by at an alarming rate, it likely means you have to "turn down the volume" on all that is coming in. The technique of 'centering' is an effective and efficient way to accomplish this. Centering is a process whereby you inhale deeply (when you are practicing place your hand on your stomach so you can feel it expand) and while inhaling mentally check the tension in your body and let it go. As you exhale feel that tension slipping away and the sense of 'heaviness' that comes with being more relaxed (if you are on your horse, feel the heaviness resulting in a 'sinking' into your saddle). Centering is an extremely effective way to take a 'time out' and then be ready to redirect your attention to a task or competitive situation. This process can be done before or during a competition (in between jumps on a course) and with practice can be accomplished in a single deep breath. Centering is also effective in shutting out internal dialogue or recovering from a break in concentration.

When you become overwhelmed:

If you find yourself in a situation where you just feel overwhelmed (you are not sure what to focus on so you keep flipping around and getting more and more frustrated) take a step back and get back to basics. In other words choose something which is simple (your position, counting your strides off), and do lots of breathing.

Focus!

*Do you need to: change the channel, eliminate
the static or turn down the volume?*

Know what gets you out of focus

Know yourself: do you have a strength in a particular area? And a weakness somewhere else? Some people get "externally overloaded" by becoming overwhelmed or confused at what to focus on in the environment. Others get "internally overloaded" or focus too much on thoughts and feelings or by overanalyzing. Finally, some athletes have trouble switching from one mode of focus to the next. (Eg: external to internal). The best defence against becoming distracted is to prepare for distraction by knowing what your weak areas are and having a plan ready to deal with them. Try to note where and when you have difficulty concentrating, and you will probably begin to discover a pattern. You can then begin to formulate a strategy to attack those weak areas.

Triggers that get me out of focus   **Re-focusing plan**

_____

_____

_____

_____

_____

_____

_____

_____

_____

Finally, it is important to remember that, as much as we would all like for the wonderful 'flow' experience to occur every day, unfortunately this is not realistic. The reality is that there are lots of ways we can become distracted during the course of a performance, and the important thing to work at is bouncing back when that happens. Fortunately, the ability to concentrate is a skill, and like any other skill, it can be improved and developed with practice.

Key Points:

• Learn what types of distractions typically get you out of focus.

• With the help of your trainer, determine what you should be focusing on.

• Practice using the strategies discussed in training to determine what refocusing plan will work best for you in competition.

Chapter
5

Managing your Butterflies

After all, our worst misfortunes never happen,
and most miseries lie in anticipation
-Honore De Balzac

What does it mean to have butterflies?

Its show time- you're at the start gate, and suddenly you become very aware of the fact that your heart is pounding rapidly, adrenaline seems to be coursing through your veins, and there is no doubt there are a swarm of butterflies slam dancing against the walls of your stomach. What's more, you just can't seem to rid yourself of the gnawing thought of having to use the bathroom just one more time... "Why, why can't I just be relaxed?", you demand of yourself, instead of having to go though this myriad of unpleasant bodily sensations.

Well, you can blame it on your inherent genetic design. The 'alarm' reaction you experience is normal and functional. Your heart rate speeds up because in order to flee from a potentially dangerous situation, your body needs blood rich in oxygen to work the muscles most effectively. We get those 'butterflies' because blood is being pumped in the direction away from the stomach and head to our muscles for immediate use. You may feel a need to run for the washroom because your body wants to er, um 'evacuate' in order to be as light and nimble as possible to face the impending danger.

The components of anxiety

As you can see, butterflies have physical and psychological components. In other words, we experience anxiety in both of these ways:

Psychological	Physical
sense of vague threat	increased heart rate
lack of confidence	increased blood pressure
worry, doubt	increased muscle tension
sense of uncertainty	feelings of nausea
inability to concentrate	frequent bathroom trips
expectations of failure	dry mouth
negative self talk	sweating, cold and clammy hands

How do you experience your butterflies? Write out what psychological and physical symptoms occur for you:

_____

_____

_____

_____

One component can impact the other. You may begin with feeling as though you have a knot in your stomach, you interpret this to mean you must be very nervous, you then begin feeling worse and your thoughts get worse and so on. This is how the cycle of worry and anxiety can get out of control and cripple your performance.

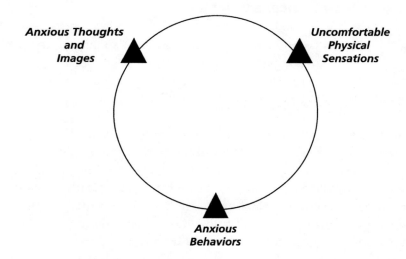

The costs of anxiety

The costs associated with excess tension can range from small interference to being debilitating to your performance. You may suffer impeded judgement, muscle control, damaged self confidence and an inability to concentrate. An overabundance of stress also causes you to be physically and or mentally drained. Have you ever noticed how tired you feel after you have experienced a period of prolonged stress? This is because we can only sustain that high physical readiness state for so long before our body is forced to replenish itself. If you often feel physically low (low energy, fatigue) and mentally tired (loss of motivation, feelings of helplessness or hopelessness), this is a signal you likely need to review how you cope with and manage your stress levels.

STRATEGIES FOR COPING

Three core skills for battling your butterflies are: managing the physical aspects, managing the psychological aspects, and teaching yourself to cope.

1) Managing the physical aspects:

Managing the physical component of butterflies means managing the state of your body. Having your body in a 'high alarm' state is of course counterproductive to your performance. In order to tone down this alarm reaction, riders need to be well versed in the skill of relaxation.

The state of relaxation is more than unwinding in front of a TV. Real relaxation involves a different physiological state characterized by a reduction in heart rate, respiration rate, blood pressure, analytical thinking, and skeletal muscle tension. Regular practice of real or deep relaxation daily produces a generalization of the relaxation response to the rest of your life. In other words, after a few weeks of practice you will find yourself being more relaxed at work, on your horse and at home. So why learn how to relax? I know you may be asking yourself this question, because relaxation is perhaps the most underrated skill among recreational and amateur athletes. Elite athletes, however, know of the value of this skill. They understand that relaxation is the foundation of all other psychological skills, such as imagery, concentration and intensity control. They also know that every change in their emotional and mental state is accompanied by a change in their bodily state. In other words, we think with our entire body, and it makes sense to learn how to regulate our own system. Research also suggests that relaxation helps us to learn better, concentrate more effectively, recover from fatigue faster and use our muscles to their complete potential. For riders, the most important benefit that comes from learning the skill of relaxation is the improvement in the feel or connection with your horse. Excess tension in your body acts as interference in the communication between you and your mount. To communicate clearly, you need to remove that interference, which can be accomplished with learning the skill of relaxation. There are several different ways you can go about learning this skill.

Breathing properly

One of the most effective ways to relax is to learn to breathe properly. Don't laugh! When you are in the grip of nervousness, trust me, you are not breathing correctly. You are most likely breathing shallowly, or from the top or upper part of your lungs. This causes you to have a lack of oxygen and before you know it you are yawning uncontrollably. Yawning is a natural defence of the body in order to ingest that much need oxygen. Look around at your next competition, see if you can spot the people who are suffering this affliction. You will see many!

Diaphragmatic breathing

To begin, sit comfortably in a chair or bed and place one hand on your stomach and one hand on your chest. I want you to be able to feel how your body reacts when you breathe the right way. If you breathe properly, you breathe from your diaphragm, or the thin muscle that separates the lung and abdominal cavities. As you inhale, you should notice that your abdomen pushes out. This is because during inhalation the diaphragm moves down slightly and this is what pushes your chest area out. As you are inhaling, it may be helpful to imagine that you are filling up three separate sections of your lungs. First, concentrate on your abdomen, making it expand with air, next fill the middle portion of your lungs by expanding the chest cavity and raising the rib cage and chest. Finally, allow the upper portion to be filled and you will notice your upper chest expand and your shoulders raise slightly. Hold your breath for several seconds before beginning the exhalation. Begin to exhale by pulling the abdomen in (this is what pulls the diaphragm up), and you should notice your shoulders drop, as well as your upper chest, as the air begins to leave your lungs. Make sure the exhalation is complete, forcing all the air out and letting go of all muscular tension as you do. (Say this silently to yourself on the exhale: "As I breathe out I let go of all the tension in my body").

For those of you who found it difficult to breathe for that count, it probably means you are still breathing too shallowly, or from your chest. If you persist, you will find it becomes easier and easier to fill your entire chest cavity with air, and breathe more deeply. As you progress with this exercise, you may extend your count to 6 on the inhale, and 7 or 8 on the exhale. This will promote an even deeper state of relaxation.

The best part of this exercise is that as you become more practiced at it, you can do it anytime, anywhere. A single deep breath can become a cue for you to relax and let go of tension, even when you are competing. It can also be used to re-focus yourself if you have become distracted by negative thoughts or something in your environment. For this reason, another term for using the single deep breath technique is 'centering'. Centering is a great way to ensure that you are breathing from your diaphragm, and getting all the necessary oxygen you need, and not breathing shallowly from your chest. If you are consistently breathing in a shallow manner it can lead to feelings of fatigue, loss of physical coordination and impairments in your concentration.

Remember that you need to practice this type of deep breathing regularly, only then can it illicit the relaxation response you desire when you are competing. If you can, I suggest getting a hold of a heart rate monitor to help you with your relaxation training. As I suggested before, real relaxation involves a physiological change, one of which is a reduction in heart rate. If you don't know anyone who has a heart rate monitor, you can always use the old fashioned method, taking your pulse from either your neck or wrist. Whatever method you use, simply take your heart rate before and after your breathing exercises. If you have truly attained a relaxed state, you should notice a reduction in your heart rate. It is helpful to chart your progress with this skill with the use of a chart:

Date	Rate tension 1 = low to 10 = high	Minutes practiced	Rate tension after practice 1 - 10

Progressive relaxation

Progressive relaxation involves alternately tensing and relaxing all the major muscle groups in your body, one at a time. The idea behind progressive relaxation is that it will enable you to detect tension and the location of that tension in your body. In other words, it can help you to become more aware of your body. Simply lay or sit down in a comfortable place and alternately tense and relax each major muscle group in your body (your facial muscles, neck, shoulders, chest, arms, hands, buttocks, thighs, calves and feet). Focus on one muscle group at a time, holding the tension long enough for you to know what tension feels like in that particular part of your body. As you then relax and let go of that tension, again, note what that feels like. As you progress through this exercise, you may find increased feelings of heaviness and warmth develop. You may also notice that you experience muscle twitches or spasms as the muscles let go of built up tension. All of this is normal.

Through the course of the exercise, you may have discovered where it is you keep most of the tension in your body. If you had trouble with the progressive relaxation, it may be that you were trying too hard. Remember that you cannot force yourself to relax, rather it is something that you allow to happen. This is an excellent exercise to practice every night before going to sleep. It is guaranteed to help you fall asleep, and with practice you will be able to spot and consequently release unwanted tension in your body during training and competition.

Relaxation exercises on horse back

I have developed a few relaxation exercises that you can do while you are riding that in my experience are effective for increasing your feel and promoting a better and more relaxed connection between you and your horse.

Progressive relaxation on horseback: After you have practiced progressive relaxation at home enough, you can also do this exercise while riding. Simply go through the same sequence of muscles, but as you do so, try holding the tension and relaxation periods longer and note how your horse responds. For example, when you tense your arm, does he react by shortening his stride, or becoming agitated? If you do this exercise enough, it can help your horse to help you detect unwanted tension in your body. In other words, if you start to notice your horse reacting in a certain way, it may be a cue for you to check for tension in a particular area.

Visualizing relaxation: This exercise involves imagining yourself riding, but thinking of your upper body and arms being made out of elastic or like a rubber band. This elastic band allows you to move with your horse, to respond in perfect harmony. You may also want to imagine your seat as being a bean bag that can form exactly to the saddle and move with your horse as it moves, with no interference.

Riding with your eyes closed: In order to truly connect to your horse and get in tune with his movement in a relaxed manner, I have found it helpful to eliminate one sense-sight. Now please bear in mind that common sense and safety dictate the success of this exercise! Only do this exercise for short periods of time, as you are headed down the length, rather than the width (or shorter area) of the arena, and make sure your horse is in a quiet and agreeable mood first. Simply close your eyes for a few strides and focus in on your horse's movement, and how well you are absorbing that movement.

Zen and the art of meditative riding

Many people worldwide have discovered and embraced eastern thought and the practice of meditation. It is not difficult to see the appeal. Slow down the pace of life and relish being in the moment. Learn to meditate and watch your stress levels drop, your health improve, and your attitude grow more positive. We long to manage our seemingly chaotic existence, to simplify and achieve peace. But can these concepts be applied to and improve your riding practice and skill? You bet they can.

Utilizing the art of meditation and skill of relaxation can help bring our awareness back to the act of riding. When you think about it, the only form of two way communication that we have with our horses is feel. We communicate by using aids - a crop, a leg or body position, a voice command. But the only way we truly know whether the intended message has been successfully received is the way our horse responds. Various elements can create static in the transmission of these messages, such as incorrectly applied skill or unforeseen circumstances. Perhaps the most common and pervasive of these interrupters are excess tension and negative self talk. Meditation and relaxation can help to alleviate these problems.

You don't need to be a Yogi or Zen Master, or even attend special classes (although they do serve to improve your practice) to benefit from the experience of meditation. What you are really after is what medical experts have coined "the relaxation response", and it is surprisingly easy to learn. Each of the following exercises can be done on horseback or off, in a comfortable place visualizing yourself riding. You may want to begin practicing off your horse until you have gained confidence in your skill.

A Riding Meditation:

Begin your riding meditation by focusing on several cycles of deep breathing until you feel your body's tension dissipate and your focus narrow. Gradually allow your focus to shift from your breath to how both you and your horse feel being in this moment together. Become aware of how your arms feel, how they connect you to your horse's mouth. Allow your awareness to travel, as though it is a ray of light. This light is soothing, and flows from the bit, through the reins, into your hands, up your forearm, past your elbow, into your biceps and finally into your shoulders. The light is comforting and allows you this beautiful connection between yourself and your horse. Notice how well he responds to you, there is a positive energy that flows between the two of you, a pure form of communication. Now imagine that this light continues to travel, down your back and into your seat. You become aware of your horses body swaying beneath you. Take a moment to feel as each hip comes forward, how your own body absorbs that movement perfectly. Now the light is travelling down into your legs, and it rests at the bottom of your heel. You now become aware of your horses sides, your legs lightly resting but still feeling the movement underneath you. You feel as though you are one entity now, completely absorbed into one being. And you will remember this feeling, this oneness, the relaxation, the sensations of your horse, your muscles, the calmness and peace and know that you can return to this state once more.

Choosing a Riding Mantra:

Some meditations involve choosing a word or phrase to focus on to guide your practice. It doesn't matter what you choose, as long as it is easy to repeat and meaningful to your riding goals. Choose a word which represents a state that you would like to promote in your riding. Some suggestions are "one", "easy", "flow", "harmony" and "fluid". Choosing a mantra simply means choosing a different point of focus for your practice instead of your breath. It should be repeated over and over during your meditation. Again, you can do this in the comfort of your own home, or while you are riding.

2) **Managing the psychological aspects**:

The most effective way to manage the psychological component of anxiety is to monitor and change your perceptions appropriately. This skill was reviewed in detail in Chapter 2. Remember that very often you can 're-frame' your anxious feelings by telling yourself your body is ready to compete. You can also be pro-active in preventing negative thoughts by consciously being prepared with positive, accurate thoughts to repeat to yourself. Reminding yourself that you have the skills to compete, and the skills to cope can be an extremely effective boost. For example, "I know I have ridden a similar course before and done well.", "I know that I have had butterflies before and been able to compete effectively. This is just my body's way of preparing myself and that means I am ready".

3) **Teaching yourself to cope**:

Experience is the greatest teacher when it comes to learning to cope with a variety of situations. The more you compete, the better you will understand and be able to manage unforeseen circumstances and difficult emotions. However, you don't have to always depend on the "trial by fire" method of learning. Using 'simulations' can be an effective shortcut.

Pilots, the military, astronauts and others all utilize simulation training. They engage in this type of training because it is the most effective way to prepare themselves apart from really being there. Not enough riders make use of this form of learning. Think about it, there is a very good reason why astronauts practice in realistic flight simulators. They have to practice using their knowledge while dealing with crisis or unexpected situations. I can guarantee they would not feel too comfortable heading out into space having only experienced it from a classroom! So why should you expect yourself to go to a show and deal effectively with competing when you have not really had practice at concentrating on riding while dealing with difficult emotions?

Schooling shows are perhaps the best example of simulation training. But if you don't have the opportunity to attend preseason competitions, try creating your own. You may want to consider approaching others in your stable and see if they would like to set up a 'mock' competition. Then all you need is some spectators (friends, parents) and someone to act as a judge if possible. Giving yourself the opportunity to 'practice' competing is an invaluable experience. Particularly in terms of your mental training. How often have you heard someone say "but I can do it at home!" What this statement actually means is: "I can do it at home because I'm not thinking about my emotions as much, but when I get to the show I'm overwhelmed!" Competing at your best is about controlling your emotions enough to let your talent shine through-and doing so is best practiced in an atmosphere which duplicates the competition environment. Below are some examples of situations that may cause stress in a competitive atmosphere which you can seek to duplicate at home:

>*Noise/crowds:* Competitive situations are often filled with activity. People milling around, excess noise, announcers booming out competitors' names. When setting up your mock show, see how well you can duplicate the noise and crowd aspects.

>*Judges/Bad judges*: Some riders have a tough time tuning out bad judging calls when they are involved in competitions in which they receive feedback about their performance but then must compete again right away. Ask your 'mock' judge to throw in a little unfairness here and there and practice coping with these evaluations.

>*Weather*: Get out there and ride in the rain and the wind. You know you will have to do it at some show at some time, so you might as well get accustomed to it.

Fatigue: So you don't feel that great today, and your considering passing on your lesson. Think again! It may be a great opportunity to see how strong your mind is when faced with an uncooperative body.

Warm-up ring chaos: Many shows do not possess the most endearing warm-up facilities. They tend to be small, noisy and confusing. You may want to consider portioning off a small section of your area and have yourself and others practice warming up effectively amid the confusion of horses and bodies.

Unexpected changes: we have all experienced the surprise of being summoned to the ring sooner than we expected, or being forced to deal with a delay when we feel warmed up and ready to compete. When staging your at-home mock show, you may want to consider having someone 'fiddle' with the original order of go.

An alternate way of conducting a simulation is to do it in your head, or to use your imagery skills. Obviously, there are some situations which are hard to recreate, such as dealing with someone trying to psych you out before you go in the ring. Using visualization, you can practice seeing yourself cope effectively with this distraction. Another advantage of imagery is that you can practice daily if you need to. If performance jitters are getting the best of you, spend ten minutes each day seeing yourself in various competition scenarios. Whether you practice in real life or in your head, simulations can help you cope with overactive butterflies.

Developing these three skills will assist you in coping with anxious feelings and sensations. In the next chapter we will consider the topic of anxiety in a little more detail. We will look at specific types of fears which commonly interfere with training and performance.

Key Points:

- Decide what method of relaxation, or combination of methods, is best for you to pursue.

- Devote a small but consistent period of time to practice (10 minutes daily)

- Consider how your thoughts may be contributing to your anxiety. Develop a plan to change your self talk in these situations.

- If there are some situations that make you nervous that you can duplicate at home in training- do it!

Chapter
6

Dealing with Different
Kinds of Fears

Assessing Your Fears

There are a myriad of reasons why we experience nervousness. What may make one person anxious may be nothing at all to another. In order to experience feelings of excessive anxiety, a person must first perceive the situation to be dangerous. A rider who is a perfectionist has fears about making mistakes, so mistakes are perceived as very dangerous and therefore produce a nervous response. Another rider may have had a series of bad crashes when jumping triple bars, so triple bars become dangerous. It is important, as stated previously, to be aware of what causes you to experience excessive stress. Otherwise, you sit facing a "wall of fear" that seems impossible to deal with. Take a look at the list of common fears below, and ask yourself what your main fears are.

Physical Fear

- Do you often think about falling off?
- Do you often think about getting hurt?
- Do you fear losing control, are you afraid to ride at a faster pace?
- Do you feel you cannot trust your horse?

Mental Fear

- Do you tend to think in 'extremes'? For example, "I rode terribly or brilliantly," "I won or I lost", "I did everything wrong today"?
- If you do not meet your goals all the time do you feel like a failure?
- Do you selectively attend to your mistakes and overlook your successes?
- Do your feelings of self-worth go up and down with your judgment of how well you have performed?
- Do you have trouble putting problems out of your mind?
- Do you tend to believe there is only one right way to do things, and if you don't do it this way, you have failed?
- When you perform does it feel as though there is a spotlight on you, and people are watching your every move and waiting for you to make a mistake?

General Worrier

- Do you have a hard time isolating what makes you fearful?
- Do you experience a low level anxiety in a lot of situations?
- Do you seem to worry too much?
- Do you always seem stressed?

Fear of Something Specific

• Do you deliberately avoid a situation (showing, oxers, riding in the rain) that makes you feel uncomfortable?

Performance Fears

• Do you ride well at home but seem to fall apart at shows?
• Do you often 'choke' when it matters most?

Write out what situations you believe "trigger" your butterflies:

_____

_____

_____

_____

_____

_____

_____

Knowing what triggers your nerves means the difference between facing a 'wall of fear' and knowing specifically what kinds of situations get your butterflies to flutter. Once you get clear on what gets you nervous, you have a much better chance of developing a plan to manage your feelings.

Know your countermoves

The reactions you experience in response to fear and anxiety will vary, but I find that there are four common ways in which people respond. All of these represent 'countermoves' or ways of seeking to escape emotional distress. Unfortunately, countermoves often lead to more problems.

> *avoidance :* These riders may avoid going out to ride, or make excuses about why they can't have a lesson or do a particular exercise. For example, I remember one young rider who was afraid to canter. Every time I instructed the group to canter, he would go into the middle of the ring and begin to fix his boots. He was avoiding the situation which produced uncomfortable feelings.

> *freezing:* This is where you may assume you can get back on and jump that oxer, but when you find yourself nearing the actual fence, you pull up. Other names for this affliction are 'numbing out' and 'blanking out'.

> *hyper vigilance:* If this is your countermove you feel jumpy and extremely conscious of every move you or your horse makes. You have convinced yourself that if you look hard enough, and often enough, you can prevent disaster from striking. If you are experiencing such a reaction, you will probably find it hard to 'let go' and just ride.

> *excessive anxiety:* The butterflies are going crazy in your stomach, your heart is pounding seemingly right through your chest and you feel as though you might pass out. It may feel very much like a panic attack.

Knowing how you now respond to the situations that create fear can help you to create the best plan of attack. With this awareness you can look for opportunities to challenge your countermoves, and break the cycle of anxiety.

What are your countermoves?

_____

_____

_____

_____

_____

_____

When I can't handle events, I let them handle themselves
-Henry Ford

Suggested strategies for different types of fears

All of the strategies reviewed in the previous chapter are useful in combating nerves. For more specific or pronounced fears, there are different strategies you can utilize. You will need to experiment with different combinations to see what works best for you. As a beginning, I have found the following combination of strategies to be most effective with the different types of fears we have discussed.

Coping with Physical Fear

If you have physical fear, you likely know it already. You may feel insecure each time you mount your horse, not knowing what may happen, whether or not you'll get hurt. For some, it's a long standing fear that they've had to battle. For others, one bad experience has knocked their confidence down, and they are struggling to rebuild. Each problem area has slightly different solutions.

Regaining Your Confidence After an Accident:

The very first thing you should do after an accident is analyze what happened. Accidents occur for many different reasons, and how you proceed to deal with it will in large part depend on this factor. Analyzing also tends to have a calming effect, as you shift into a logical mode of thinking as opposed to an emotional one. As mentioned, there are numerous reasons why accidents occur. Many, many accidents happen to athletes and in general because of preoccupation with other life stressors. These stressors may include marital discord, school difficulties, life transition (graduation or marriage), financial difficulties and other 'life changing' events. So ask yourself - have there been things going on in your life that may be draining all your energy and concentration? Other times accidents occur because we just lack good common sense (ie.: "I knew my horse was incredibly fresh after a week off but I just got on him anyway"). It also could be that you were attempting a task which was over your skill level, or that you got a little too overconfident and took a risk with very poor odds and you happened to lose. Sometimes, of course, we simply guilty of being mindless! Unfortunately there is no way you can escape this condition, unless of course you happen to be inhuman. The point is, you can ease a lot of fear if you carefully go through what happened, and what's more you may discover it may only be a matter of correcting a very obvious mistake.

One of the worst things you can do after an accident is to deny your feelings and play the "tough cookie" routine. If you deny your feelings you could be setting yourself up to do more damage. This is a situation I have seen many times and experienced myself. If you ignore what happened, and begin before you are psychologically prepared, the ensuing tentativeness or overcompensating boldness could lead to another injury or a further loss of confidence. Sure, you have to have some degree of 'mental toughness', or be able to push through some fear and apprehension. Just make sure you are doing it for the right reasons (remember, you don't need to be anybody's hero but your own), and that your outlook is tempered with some common sense. You should also take care to ensure that you are adequately physically prepared before you begin riding again. I'm not suggesting that you wait until you are 100%, but rather that you assess how your injury will affect your riding. For instance, if it is the type of injury that will affect your balance, and you begin too soon, again you may be asking for another accident to happen or risk losing confidence in your skills.

How you begin to build up your confidence after an accident will depend on your unique situation and your individual personality. Some of the factors which will make your situation unique include: age, experience level, coach, urgency of situation (competition), presence/absence of injury, injury type/severity and previous falls. It may take some time to sort out the best approach for you, or if it feels overwhelming, you may want to invest in some outside help.

If you have a long standing physical fear:

If you have a nagging physical fear that just wont go away, you will have to step back and ask yourself a few questions:

- Are you overfaced? (are you being asked to do things which overwhelm you on a regular basis? If so, let your trainer know immediately)
- Are you over mounted? (Is your horse too hot, or in some other way not suited to your ability or our personality?
- How are your physical skills developing? Are you stuck somewhere in your learning process and need to redefine your goals?
- Are you stuck because of a specific incident? Was there an accident in the past that is still impacting your learning and performance?

Techniques and Suggestions for Rebuilding your Physical Confidence:

Take it slow: unless you have an impending competition, it is a good idea to take things slow when you resume riding. This may also mean 'bumping down a notch' in terms of what you do in lessons, such as jumping smaller jumps or not riding without stirrups.

Build physical strength/basic skills: to increase your sense of physical security, you may want to really concentrate on building your physical strength. You don't necessarily need to ride for this, although you can. It can be just as effective for you to go to the gym and work on those legs! In terms of focusing on basic skills, like body position etc. this can not only increase your sense of security on a horse, but also give you something positive to focus your attention on.

Realign your self talk: when we experience anxiety, we are always conveying certain messages to ourselves. You may not be aware that you are sending yourself messages like "I know I will fall off again if I try that fence" or "I cant ride at all, whatever possessed me to think I could!?" If you catch yourself talking in your head like this, tell yourself- 'STOP!' and then replace those thoughts with more reasonable, positive ones. For example: "STOP. I am feeling a little bit anxious about riding again, but that's normal and I can still ride with that anxiety. I am feeling more confident riding everyday." If you are having trouble with the strength of your negative thoughts try this exercise: pretend you are a lawyer and you are being asked to refute a belief (your negative self statement) by gathering and presenting all the evidence to the contrary (ie.: what exactly is the probability that you will fall off again, given the facts of the situation?). This approach is not only effective in terms of getting you logically, as opposed to emotionally oriented, but also has the tendency to inject some much needed humour into the situation!

Visualize yourself correcting the problem: if you have discovered that the accident was indeed due to a technical error, then you can visualize yourself performing correctly. One big caution with this: make sure you do find out, from a coach preferably, what exactly it was you should have been doing (like shifting your weight to the outside when riding a corner) and concentrate on that in your imagery sessions. You cannot effectively visualize by telling yourself "now I see myself not doing that", because the brain cannot process 'not' very well and usually goes with the doing that part of the statement (ask yourself, what does 'not' shifting my weight to the inside when riding a corner look like?).

Relaxation training: there are lots of people who are not even aware they have excess tension in their body, and as everyone knows, this can have a really adverse impact on your horse's confidence as well as your own.

Tell your Trainer: It is helpful to let your trainer or coach know how you feel. If you don't, they may not know how you are feeling inside and be instructing you to do things which feel dangerous to you and increase your anxiety.

Coping with Mental Fear

Emma sat slumped over in her saddle anxiously awaiting her next turn in the lesson. A million thoughts raced through her head: "I can't believe I got my pace all wrong again! I always do this, I can't figure this out, I must be a terrible rider, I'm not cut out for this!". What's worse, her trainer had again barked at her for 'shaking her head' in self-disgust as she had finished the last fence. "You have a terrible attitude!" she had yelled, "I had better not catch you doing that at a show unless you want to draw the judges and everyone else's attention to your mistake!" Emma had cringed inside at that word - "MISTAKE", she felt dejected and tired, and very much like a failure.

Riders who are perfectionists feel as though they are in a kind of spotlight all the time. This harsh glare cruelly seeks to reveal the smallest of errors, under the most intense magnification. These riders tend to feel a missed lead change or botched fence will end up as headline news, making them suffer incredible humiliation. Due to these significant pressures, many perfectionists will do everything within their power to stop mistakes from happening in the first place. They expend enormous amounts of energy trying to avoid errors, often by "what ifing" themselves to death.

It should come as no surprise that riders who have this tendency also risk jeopardizing the effective training of themselves and their mounts. Because they are overly 'cautious' they tend to shield themselves and their horses from mistakes in much the same way an overprotective parent shields their children from potential harm. If horses, like people, are not given opportunities to learn to cope, then when unexpected events occur they end up, well, lost.

How to lessen the costs of having a perfectionist personality:

Learn to set more reasonable goals for yourself: Take a piece of paper and write out your goals.. Next take a good hard look at these and ask yourself whether they are reasonable, attainable goals. You may want to ask others what their opinion is, if you are not sure how to evaluate for reasonableness. How much success will these goals allow you to feel? If your goals are only about winning and losing, you are setting yourself up to feel discouraged a lot more than you will feel encouraged. One question you may ask yourself is: what is my definition of success? Spend some time reflecting on this question, asking yourself not only what you believe about success but whether or not you live these beliefs. I have seen many riders say "I am not that hard on myself", but their actions prove differently.

Get conscious about your expectations: Conduct an experiment. Spend one day trying to be ultra conscious of what your expectations are in any given situation. Are you really allowing yourself to make mistakes and to be human? Are you expecting that you should be able to be in control at all times? Take a good hard look at how you are evaluating yourself and how often.

Build your tolerance to mistakes: Experiment with making mistakes deliberately, and coaching yourself through the 'aftermath'. Perfectionists often have problems coping with unforeseen difficulty. You can teach yourself to cope better with mistakes by either visualizing yourself making a mistake and then coping with it in an effective, problem solving way, or by actually looking for those opportunities to challenge yourself in training. For example, if you have a fear of riding at a faster pace because this feels out of control, and like a "mistake" to you, challenge yourself to ride at an exaggerated pace at home in training until you 'desensitize' yourself to this fear. Remember that you will also be training your horse to cope better as well.

Strive to be more accepting of yourself: Perfectionists have a tough time accepting themselves as they are. They always feel they should be striving and struggling to be a certain way. Ask yourself this question: "if I was 1% more accepting of myself today I would..." and then finish the statement as many times as you can. Your list may look something like this: "if I was 1% more accepting of myself today I would...1)be a little less worried and better able to focus on my horse, 2) I would smile more because I would feel more at ease, 3) I would be a little less sensitive to criticism from my coach.

Check your focus: Make sure you train yourself to focus on the task before you, not on avoiding a mistake. If you find your mind wandering to what may go wrong, bring yourself back to the here and now by giving yourself an easy cue such as "now" or "be here". Alternatively, you may cue yourself back to what task you should be focusing on such as "pace" or "eyes forward". Furthermore, remember that when all your energy goes to avoiding trouble you may actually bring it on yourself.

Another tip regarding focus: perfectionists, when at the height of anxiety, tend to develop a very narrow focus which highlights every detail of possible failure. Many riders I have worked with find it helpful to switch their focus from themselves to what they are doing to make their horses learn better and perform better. This takes the glare off themselves and puts their focus on practical matters.

Monitor your self talk or "internal dialogue": What are your common perfectionistic "mental ruts"? Thinking in black and white terms (I win or I lose), catastrophizing (making mountains out of mole hills), or 'negative filter' (discounting all that is positive). Strive to cultivate a kinder, more gentler voice inside your head that says its enough for you to do the best that you can, and to make a few mistakes along the way.

One word of caution as you embark on your changes. When perfectionists try to be more forgiving of themselves there tends to be this little voice that goes off in their head that says "lazy, you are just being lazy", or "there you go, sluffing off again". You must consider this voice to be the enemy! Try to remember that change comes about as a result of many small steps. Be patient with yourself, striving for subtle shifts in your thinking that will one day add up to good habits. As a final note, perfectionist riders tend to be perfectionists - period. That is, their beliefs often show their impact in other areas of their life. If you commit to change in this area, you should notice the benefits in your overall happiness, as well as your riding pleasure.

If you are a general worrier:

There are people who have inherited an 'anxious personality', or have developed a habit of worry. They may have difficulty articulating what makes them nervous, and detecting tension within their body. Some of the biggest indicators of an anxious personality can be felt in the body. Watch for feelings of fatigue that never seem to go away, or a tendency to yawn or sigh frequently. Jennifer is one such rider. She often feels on the verge of being drained. "I always seem to lack energy, even though I think I'm fit. Other people tell me I look tired and slump a lot. I know it has to do with the way that I think. I spend a lot of time and energy thinking about everything that could go wrong."

Breaking the cycle of worry:

Remind yourself that worry does not equal control: Many worriers have falsely convinced themselves that if they do worry, this will somehow prevent the worst from happening. When you catch yourself engulfed in worry, stop yourself. Then ask, 'what am I worried about?' Is it a controllable or non controllable factor? If it is uncontrollable, like poor judging, then park it. If it's controllable, like worry about your horse being too fresh, then develop a concrete plan to deal with the problem. Get used to challenging the worry, and separating it into accept and action items. You accept what you cannot change, you take action whenever possible.

Separate your worry into 'Accept' and 'Action' items

Use affirmations to put you into the right mindset: Deliberately chose statements which will help you maintain your focus. For example, 'I am clear and calm', or 'I am focused on the tasks before me'.

Learn to control your physical sensations: Consider yoga, meditation or other formal instruction in relaxation. If you are a worrier type, you need to make lifestyle changes that will support you in your goal to 'let go'.

Put a "stop-loss" order on your worries. Decide just how much anxiety a thing may be worth - and refuse to give it any more
-Dale Carnegie

101

Have a clear plan to deal with your fears

If you fear something specific

If you become anxious in response to a particular situation (water jumps for example), then you have what is called situational anxiety. If however, you begin to avoid water jumps altogether, it can then be said that you have a phobia. In other words, phobias involve persistent avoidance of a particular situation.

But how do anxieties and phobias form in the first place? Fears are something which we learn. The type of learning that is associated with the development of phobias is called Classical Conditioning and in most simple terms can be thought of as learning by association. An example will explain this more effectively, and the best example is still the first experiment ever performed to illustrate this type of learning: Pavlov's dogs. Russian physiologist Ivan Pavlov discovered that the dogs participating in his digestion studies began to salivate as soon as they saw the experimenter, because they had come to associate him with the meat powder they were fed for the experiment. In short, the dogs had paired or associated the food with the experimenter, so that over time only the experimenter elicited the salivation response. The dogs had learned an association. There are many examples of this type of learning in horses. For example, a loud noise naturally produces a startle response in a horse. If whenever you ride by a door in the arena, and the wind blows and rattles the door and your horse spooks, it is possible that your horse will spook at all doors because he has generalized that response to a particular stimulus-the door. So instead of the door rattling producing the spook response, now the door itself elicits the same response because it has become associated with the same event.

So this is how phobias are learned, by association. If you have had a tendency to crash at oxers, before long your mind associates crashing with oxers and viola, oxer phobia is born. The good news is, there are ways to 'undo' this type of learning. The way you unlearn a phobia or association is by pairing the event with a different outcome, thereby learning a 'new' association. For example, if you want to eliminate your oxer phobia, you want to replace your fear reaction with a different one, like relaxation. If you were to go and see a psychologist about this problem, they would likely use something called 'systematic desensitization'. There are four stages to the systematic desensitization process:

Relaxation training: The first step involves the psychologist teaching deep relaxation. This stage usually lasts until the relaxation response can be elicited by a cue such as taking a deep breath and saying "I am relaxed". It is important that the relaxation response be strong for the rest of the treatment to be effective.

Constructing an anxiety scale: The individual and the therapist would then construct a scale of anxiety producing events, ordered on the basis of how much anxiety they evoke. To be most effective, the items should be equidistant in terms of the anxiety they illicit. In other words, you wouldn't want an event which evokes a 1 on an anxiety scale from 1 to 10, followed by an item which then elicits a 7 on the same scale. Usually the scale of events will contain about 10 to 15 items, but may be smaller. Using our oxer phobia example, a the first or least anxiety provoking event may be cantering over two poles laid over the ground to form an oxer, and at the other end of the scale, cantering to a full size oxer from a tight corner. I am reluctant to present you with a full example, as two people with the same phobia may have entirely different scale formations.

Desensitization: This stage involves the individual first being led through relaxation, and then asked to image the anxiety provoking event. Again, with the example of the oxer phobia, we would begin with the least feared item, and have the person visualize themselves performing this event. If there is a hint of anxiety during this image, the visualization is halted, and there is a return to the relaxation process. This continues until the individual can image the event without anxiety. Then the next item on the scale will be presented and the same process followed until all the items on the scale have been covered. It may take anywhere from five to ten sessions to complete this process, at times longer as sometimes revisions have to be made to the scale.

In Vivo Desensitization: 'In vivo' basically means 'live' or 'in real life' and involves confronting the feared event in real life. This stage is also highly structured, usually involving facing only those situations which have been covered in the visualization stage, and again returning to the relaxation response should anxiety arise.

As you can see, what this process does is replace the learned response (fear) with a different one (relaxation). This type of treatment has been shown to be highly successful with simple, or less complex fears. For this reason I feel I need to offer a word of caution at this point. The aforementioned technique of systematic desensitization is one usually done with the guidance of a professional. If you have a fairly simple fear, you may try to use these steps, beginning with relaxation (taking the time to ensure you can illicit the relaxation response), construction of the scale, the visualization and, if appropriate, the 'live' test.

If you are plagued by a phobia, its important to first remember that it is not the thing that you fear, its your perception of the thing. In other words, its not the dog, its not the oxer, its not the snake or the elevator. What you actually come to fear is the feeling of anxiety, and this is what directs you to avoid that thing, and the reward you get from doing so is an absence of anxiety. Unfortunately, this is the only advantage to avoidance, otherwise it usually holds you back from things you would like to do. The good news is phobias are highly treatable with strategies like systematic desensitization.

> ***Do thing you fear, and the death of fear is certain***
> ***–Ralph Waldo Emerson***

Performance Fears

While everyone is plagued by performance jitters to some extent, for other riders it becomes a debilitating affliction. Kelly is one such example. She excels in her skill development at home, her trainer is extremely pleased with her progress. However, Kelly at a show is a different person altogether. It was easy to tell just by looking at her. She seemed absorbed in her own world and it was often difficult to communicate with her. As her anxiety grew, Kelly would predictably end up choking and pulling up or making unnecessary circles in the ring.

The challenge with performance fears is figuring out exactly what they are all about. Our stress naturally escalates when we go to compete, as we perceive the event to be 'more important' which of course it is. While the weight of the importance of the event may get out of hand for some, for others there are different explanations for their nerves. See below for what is surely the beginning of a very long list:

- making a mistake in public
- letting someone down
- not having confidence in your riding ability
- fear of fear and it's effects
- worrying about what others will think of you

So your first step is to do what it takes to figure out what aspects of performing make you most anxious. You can accomplish this through deduction, a little observation and perhaps even asking others to watch your responses and provide feedback. Once you have weeded the culprit out, develop an appropriate strategy. For example, Kelly discovered that she was afraid of what her body felt like when it was preparing to compete. She had always assumed that the sensations she experienced were negative and would certainly lead to more trouble. Once she realized that this was her body's natural and necessary way of preparing itself, she felt normal for the first time. From this point she was able to work at managing the state of her body through relaxation and as a result was able to feel in control of her riding once more.

Now that you have a clearer understanding of your 'trigger situations', identify your plan of action for combating your fears:

_____

_____

_____

_____

_____

_____

_____

Key Points:

- Define your fears as clearly as you can. Work on one at a time.

- Know your 'countermoves', watch for opportunities to challenge them.

- Define a specific plan to tackle each fear, using the strategies discussed.

- Make sure your plan is focused on controllable, vs. uncontrollable factors.

Chapter
7

Managing your Intensity Level

Or what having "good anxiety" means...

What is intensity?

You have likely heard people talk about good stress and bad stress. Many find these discussions confusing. You have likely asked yourself, what can be good about stress? Why should I have to feel that way, if its so uncomfortable? And, you would be right.

The truth is, anxiety does impede performance and is negative. When we look to define anxiety, we look to the psychological components of 'butterflies' listed in chapter 5. Anxiety has to do with all of these things: negative statements, lack of confidence and excessive worry or doubt. Clearly these are aspects we could do without in trying to be successful competitors.

What people commonly refer to as 'good stress' may more accurately be called 'intensity'. Intensity has to do with being psychologically and physically stimulated enough to perform a task to the best of our ability. When you possess 'intensity' you do experience some of the symptoms associated with butterflies: increased respiration rate, increased blood pressure, increased muscle tension, increased perspiration, increased heart rate and elevated levels of adrenaline. The difference lies in your perception of what is occurring in your body, and in the quality of your mood. So instead of interpreting those butterflies to mean "I'm nervous", if you feel them as intensity you perceive them to mean "I'm ready". Rather than your mood being low or anxious, you are energized and excited.

So there is a difference between feelings of nervousness and those of intensity or anticipation. However, many riders make the mistake of thinking that feelings of anxiety and intensity are the same. In other words, if my heart is beating more rapidly then I must be nervous. This may only mean that your body is physically preparing for the challenge-a natural response. It doesn't have to mean that you are anxious which, as we have seen, tends to have more to do with feelings of worry or doubt about your performance. But all this begs the question, how much intensity do you need to perform well and how do you get it?

Finding your optimal intensity level

Early research insisted that the relationship between intensity and peak performance was a straight, linear one. In other words, that the higher your intensity level, the better the performance. Today, however, researchers believe the relationship to be more curvilinear in nature. That is, too low an intensity level is undesirable, as is too high an intensity level. The "optimal" range therefore falls somewhere between these two extremes, or where intensity is in the moderate range. The optimal range, however, also changes with respect to some other factors:

What kind of sport you are in: In general, the more physically complex the task, the lower intensity level needed. For example, a power lifter does not have to worry about reacting to others, or to unexpected events in the environment. They only have to concentrate on the sequence of lifting, a task of sheer power. Therefore power lifters require a high degree of intensity, or have a need to be 'really psyched up.' By contrast, a target shooter or golfer needs to process more information, and operates best under a low level of intensity. You can imagine how difficult it would be to aim at a target accurately if you were all wound up!

Although no formal research has been completed, it seems reasonable to assume that riders would fall somewhere between these two extremes in terms of their optimal level of intensity. The task of riding can be fairly complex, and requires that a considerable amount of information be processed, and yet strength is a factor. Jumper riders would naturally aim for higher levels of intensity than hunter or dressage riders. Barrel-racers and bare-back riders higher still. Keep in mind these are simply common sense generalizations that can be useful in formulating an optimal range.

Your personality: What is your own personality profile? Low key? High? If you are a low key person, you may have to work hard to get yourself psyched up and thus your optimal range would be higher. If you are a low key person involved in a relatively low intensity sport (dressage), then perhaps you naturally are at the right level of intensity. But if you are a high key person who is a dressage rider, then all your work will be directed at 'bringing yourself down' to the correct level of intensity needed to perform at your best.

Your horse: Of course it goes without saying that horses have intensity levels all their own. If you ride a "hot" horse, then you adjust your level of intensity or energy accordingly (down). In short, the personality of your mount can have an impact on your target level of intensity.

Perhaps the best route to determining your optimal range is to look at past and worst performances. During these times you performed at your best, what was the state of your body and mind? How about when you were at your worst? Ask yourself the following questions, and a pattern should emerge that tells you what helps and hinders you achieving the right state.

What did your body feel like? Was there evidence of low level butterflies, how much muscle tension was present?

Best:

_____

_____

_____

_____

Worst:

_____

_____

_____

_____

What did your horse feel like? Don't discount the horse factor! All riders know there is an exchange of energy that occurs between themselves and their mount. Did you work him early in the morning before your class, lunge him? Was he quiet and responsive or a little 'revved' and responsive?

Best:

_____

_____

_____

_____

Worst:

_____

_____

_____

_____

What were your thoughts? Did you remind yourself of anything in particular before going into the ring? What were your thoughts focused on?

Best:

_____

_____

_____

_____

Worst:

_____

_____

_____

_____

Miscellaneous factors: Who was present or not? Family, trainers, friends?

Best:

_____

_____

_____

_____

Worst:

_____

_____

_____

_____

Given these factors, what do you think your 'optimal range' looks like? You can think about this in terms of aiming at a target from 1=low intensity to 10=high intensity. Assign a number to your optimal range. This is what you will be aiming for. Imagine what you look like when you are in this state. Spend a few minutes visualizing this, and then write out your number, and your description for your optimal range. If you are involved in a horse sport (three day eventing, pentathlon) that requires different intensity levels, identify a target range for each phase.

_____

_____

_____

_____

_____

_____

_____

_____

_____

Regulation of your intensity level

We have already examined strategies for lowering tension and anxiety that will be useful in regulating your optimal intensity range. But what do you do if you need to 'psych up' in order to get to your optimal range? If you find you need to increase your energy level, here are a few techniques you can try:

Energizing techniques:

1.   A good hard and fast rule is: walk, talk and smile. These activities naturally elevate your heart rate and are easy to do.

2.   Develop key phrases that you can say to yourself ("psych up!", "charge!", "go!" etc.)

3.   Change your self talk to reflect the state you are striving for. Try affirmations like: "I am strong and ready", "I am energized", "I am alert and focused". Create an affirmation that is most meaningful to you.

4.   Visualize a scene or perhaps an animal that suggests energy to you. (For example, a thunderstorm, a tiger)

5.   Use music to change your mood and energy. Choose some upbeat techno, Latin - whatever gets you going, and put it in your walkman to listen to before your class.

6.   Turn your emotions into energy. With a little practice, you can turn seemingly negative emotions into energy. For example, feelings of fear, anticipation and anger, with the help of a little perception change, can be turned into passion for your performance.

Use music to help you energize before a competition

You may need to experiment with what amount of energy you generally require to produce a winning performance. Through this process, you may also find that you require slightly different levels according to the situation. There may be times when you need to fluctuate your intensity level during the course of a performance. One example is that of a derby class, where you may have a need to be aggressive at times, and then come down and conserve your energy for the next difficult section of the course. Keep in mind that you cannot sustain a high level of energy or intensity on an ongoing basis, as sooner or later your body will say "stop!" and begin to shut down on its own. Unfortunately this tends to feel negative, and be interpreted as "I'm too weak". If you take control over your energy, you will spare yourself this experience. When you take charge, you can then decide when its appropriate to come down, not your body!

One technique that has proven helpful is to learn to visualize your energy or intensity level as a thermometer or gauge that you can check and regulate. If your fuel is too low, plan to energize, if its too high, plan to relax.
In sum, achieving an optimal level of intensity is indeed a complex issue. But as we have seen, it is made easier by having an awareness of the demands of your particular sport, your personality your horse, and analyzing past performances.

Visualize your intensity level as a gauge
that you can check and regulate

Key Points:

- Remind yourself that a certain amount of physiological arousal, though at times uncomfortable, is necessary for peak performance.

- Assess your intensity level requirements according to the factors discussed in this chapter.

- Practice regulating your intensity level at home in training.

- Have a easily executable plan ready for competition time that will assist you in getting to your peak state.

Part Two

TRAINING
&
COMPETITION

Chapter
8

Making the Most of Your Training Time

*It's not necessarily the amount of time you spend at practice
that counts; it's what you put into the practice.*
—Eric Lindros

Making the most of your training time involves learning consciously and efficiently, having a plan and having the means to evaluate that plan. Training is about learning, practicing and refining both your physical skills and your mental skills. It's where all the hard work (and fun) take place, compared to that round at the horse show that takes mere minutes to complete!

To Learn: to gain knowledge or understanding of or skill in,
by study, instruction or experience. To come to be able
and to come to realize, to come to know, to acquire
knowledge, skill or a behavioural tendency.
-Webster's New Collegiate Dictionary

Learning Efficiently:

Although the above definition is simple and straightforward, the process of learning can appear at times to be mysterious and complex. Especially when it comes to learning a new riding skill, which can be tedious and frustrating, and it may seem as if we will never get it right. So what does it take to learn a skill, and how can you maximize this learning process? To begin with, there are three basic components involved in learning a new skill:

1) The "Thinking" Stage:

When you are first attempting to learn a skill, the focus is on gaining an understanding of how that skill is to be performed. Your trainer or coach will likely explain, and perhaps even demonstrate how to perform the skill. They are also likely to instruct you on how to "talk" your way through the skill sequence. For example, in order to get your horse to turn left, the instructions might be: "hold your right rein steady, and open up your left rein as if to guide him to the left. Apply pressure with your right leg to move him to the left." This way, you are left with a series of step by step instructions that you can use to 'talk' your way through the skill performance. These series of instructions may at first be quite simplistic, as in the example above, or just enough to get you through the basic sequence. As this sequence is mastered, however, a more sophisticated set of instructions may replace the first, giving you more control over your performance of the skill. This first phase is also characterized by the use of vision to help you in your skill acquisition. That is, you are likely to be watching your legs, hands etc. as they perform the skill. For a good example of why this is try recalling how you first learned to bounce a ball when you were a young child. At first you had to carefully watch both your hand and the ball in order to make contact. If you looked away, you were likely to miss the ball entirely. In short, at this stage of skill acquisition you are very conscious of your movements and must devote your full attention to them. That is why a good rule of thumb at this stage is "one thing at a time". Decide what it is you must focus on, and let the rest go, otherwise it is likely you will become 'overloaded' and end up frustrated. The "thinking" phase is a relatively short period in the overall learning process. It may be as brief as a few minutes for a simple skill, such as learning to hold your reins, or longer in the learning of a complex skill. This stage is complete once the skill can be performed in its entirety, and you are ready to begin practicing.

In the initial stages of learning remember to keep things simple, as you have a need to take in information more slowly and consciously

2) The "Connection" Stage:

This stage is largely about practicing and perfecting, eliminating any movements you don't need. As you practice, you will find yourself being less conscious of your execution of the skill. That is to say that you will be "thinking" less and operating more on the "feeling" level. In other words, you will begin to be able to tell when you are off simply by how it feels, and you will no longer have to look to see whether you have your leg in the right place or what your hands are doing. A great example of this is when you first learn how to get the right diagonal when you are doing a posting or rising trot. At first you have to look to see when your horse's shoulder is coming forward, but after awhile you are able to feel it, and later still you just do it automatically without even thinking consciously about it. This stage can last anywhere from a few hours to a few months for more complex skills. Near the end of this stage you should have mastered the skill to the point where you can now attend to other aspects of your performance while doing the skill. What this means is that you can now begin to do "two things at once". Returning to the example of the child learning to bounce a ball, at this stage that child could not only dribble the ball without looking at it, but also could start to devote some attention to trying to run or move with the ball at the same time.

In the second stage, concentrate on how the skill feels

3) The "Flow" Stage:

This phase is characterized by being able to perform that skill at a maximum level of proficiency. You should also now be able to perform the skill automatically, or without consciously thinking about it. In fact, at this stage verbal cues or attention to muscle movement often results in a disruption of the skill execution. I'm sure you have all had the experience where you start to 'over think' what you are doing and suddenly your performance seems to fall apart. One way of thinking about this stage is that the skill has become "programmed" into your automatic repertoire. In the flow stage you are free to direct your attention to other aspects of your performance. It should be noted that in order to keep the skill at this level you still require practice or the sequence may become rusty. It is not uncommon to lose some level of performance when attempting to 're-discover' a skill because you have to shift back into your 'thinking' mode temporarily. However, once your re-learning is complete, your performance should be even better.

When you have mastered the skill, careful not to over think as you could be stuck in "paralysis by analysis"

Practice is obviously important throughout the learning process. However, practice alone does not make perfect. In order to really improve, you must be motivated to learn. This motivation in turn is what gives your practice meaning. If the intent to learn is not there, some learning may occur, but improvement rarely does. In addition to being motivated, you must also learn mindfully. By being mindful I mean being aware of your learning process. I say this because it is possible to learn something well, but its use to you is nothing. So you also have to think while you are learning: why am I learning this?, is this working?, is this getting me my desired result?

Finally, the entire learning process is enhanced by staying positive and realistic. This is where your mental skills can make a difference. Stay positive by encouraging yourself in your learning and avoiding self-talk like "I know I will never be able to do this". Stay realistic by reminding yourself that acquiring a new skill takes time and patience. At first you can expect to fumble around and feel awkward, but this is only temporary. So go easy on yourself and remember that each skill you already possess and are able to perform flawlessly began this way.

The only place where success comes before work is in the dictionary.
—Vidal Sassoon

Becoming a "Thinking Rider"

What distinguishes a thinking rider from well, a non-thinking one? To begin with, a thinking rider is a mindful rider. Mindfulness, according to psychologist Ellen Langer, is a state of mind in which we are in the present, actively drawing distinctions, generating options and asking questions. In other words, when we are mindful, we are alert and focused, challenging incoming information to see whether it can help us to solve problems or improve our skills. Professional riders are thinking riders. They can't go into a competition thinking "I sure hope this works out today". They have to have developed a strategy from the knowledge of months or years of training and be prepared to carry it out. Thinking riders also take responsibility for their own progress, and have developed a problem solving orientation. They are constantly evaluating and reevaluating the merits of their plan or strategy to see whether they are meeting their goals. Further, they realize that there is always more than one way to accomplish an objective, and welcome creative options. Most coaches would agree, thinking riders are very 'coachable' riders and they learn faster and more effectively.

Have you ever been guilty of mindless behaviour? Well, lets see. Have you ever: come out of a round thinking "what did I just do?", gone off course, assumed that you could not do something (a course, a skill, a jump) because in the past you were unable to do it, make the same mistake again and again, assume there was only one solution to a problem or done something because it was the 'way somebody else did it'. In order to develop yourself as a thinking rider, you need to: take steps to increase your awareness, take responsibility, and actively learn to be a problem solver.

Increase your awareness:

Mindless behaviour is characterized by a lack of awareness, or just allowing things to happen. Remember that awareness is the essence of mindful behaviour. One easy way to increase your personal awareness is by asking yourself, or if you are a coach, asking your students questions which provoke thought and challenge self knowledge.

When I was teaching riding lessons, it suddenly dawned on me that here I was saying "put your heels down", "don't let him drop his shoulder in that corner" and 'do this flat exercise" and my students didn't really know why in a lot of cases I was asking them to do these things. They were just mindlessly following my instructions and getting through the lessons, sometimes things would work out, sometimes not. After I realized this, I began to teach quite differently. I wanted them to think about why the exercises and skills I asked them to practice were important, and in what other context they could use this knowledge to solve a problem. So I began asking questions to test their knowledge, and using exercises in one part of the lesson that could be used in the over fences portion of the lesson to help solve a course problem. I also left time at the end of lessons specifically for questions, encouraging their queries as much as I could. The effect of this approach was that everyone woke up, stopped ridding around in a daze and were a lot more alert. They also became more interested in their riding. The questions I asked about riding skills and exercises were designed to promote physical or technical awareness and knowledge, but I also asked questions to increase psychological awareness. For example, I might say "you did that last exercise really well, how did you prepare yourself mentally, and what helped you to concentrate so well that time?"

Take responsibility:

Thinking athletes are responsible athletes. Riders who take responsibility for themselves are the kind of riders who know that their progress is dependent upon themselves, and not a trainer or coach. They are continually working toward knowing how to take care of their own needs, whether this involves being able to look after oneself at a horse show in the absence of a coach or trainer.

Learn to be a problem solver:

Taking action involves generating options and problem solving. Putting all the pieces of the puzzle together and trying out a solution.

The number one benefit of becoming a problem solving, thinking rider is that you increase your confidence. If I was asked to provide a definition of self esteem I would have to say it involves having experiences whereby you challenge yourself and discover that you can cope and get better.

You will never "find" time for anything. If you want time you must make it
-Charles Buxton

Tracking your Progress

The act of journalling or keeping a diary is one which has become increasingly popular. Many find it an excellent way to get out difficult feelings, explore new possibilities or provide perspective. The act of writing your thoughts and feelings down can be beneficial in a number of different ways. Journals or diaries can also be kept for different reasons other than personal growth. Many top athletes employ the use of 'sport journals' in order to help their performance, but you don't need to be a professional athlete to reap the benefits of journalling. Keeping a sport journal allows you to record valuable information that can assist you in reaching your physical and mental goals. It can also be a place where you record and work through difficult feelings. All you need to get started is the notebook of your choice, and the discipline to fill it in!

There are many ways you can organize your journal: by day, training session, or before and after training. Experiment to see what works best for you. Below are some ideas/questions you may want to include in your diary:

1. **Stressors:** What situations usually cause you stress? (parents watching, disagreement with coach, thinking someone else is better than you, making a mistake etc.) How do you experience this stress? (What kind of thoughts, what do you do, what does your body feel like?) What techniques do you use to manage your stress and how effective are you at controlling it?

2. **Relationships:** How are you getting along with your coach, parents, or others that are involved closely with you and your riding? Do you tend to have frequent disagreements? About what? How do you usually respond and feel?

3. **Self-talk:** You may want to keep track of how many or what kind of negative thoughts you tend to have in training and/or competition. What is the situation, what are the thoughts and what kind of action do those thoughts cause you to take? When you are feeling more positive about your riding, what kind of thoughts do you tend to have then?

4. **Evaluation of progress:** How are your goals progressing? How will you know when its time to re-evaluate a goal? What is your greatest psychological strength, and weakness? (what do you do really well, and what area needs the most improvement)

5. **Emotions:** How are you at controlling your emotions? Do you tend to get angry frequently, or feel like giving up? Are you anxious a lot of the time or just in response to certain situations? What about other emotions, when do you notice you are excited, happy or feel challenged?

6. **Confidence:** What is your confidence level like right now? What causes it to change? Are there times when you feel more confident? If so, what is happening? You may also want to ask others (coach, friends) what they notice about you when you are confident.

7. **Peak Performance:** What does it feel like when you perform at your best? What do you feel/think during the warm-up, directly before and after the competition? What is your energy level like? How does your body feel? What was your attitude toward the competition? How did your horse feel and what did you do to get him to that state?

Find time to track your progress

As you have probably figured out, there can be many advantages to keeping a sport journal. You can keep track of your progress, release unwanted tension, work through difficulties, sharpen your focus and uncover harmful patterns that may be holding you back. Probably the greatest benefit in keeping a sport journal is that it tends to increase your awareness. Because you are writing things down, you begin to be more conscious of what is working, or not working with respect to your performance. This aspect of journalling is invaluable, as no change can ever take place without first an awareness of where you are right now.

Instead of keeping a journal, you could take a more structured approach. Below are some helpful questions you can ask yourself on a regular basis during training. You can either write out your thoughts or keep 'mental' notes.

1. What were your stressors for today's lesson? (Example: I made a bad mistake, my parents were watching etc.)

2. How did you experience this stress? (What kind of thoughts, what did you do, what did your body feel like?)

3. What techniques did you use to manage your stress and how effective were you at controlling it?

4. How was your self-talk? (What kinds of things were you saying to yourself)

5. What did you learn today that could be useful in the future (specific strategies that worked, or didn't work for you.

6. Describe what you enjoyed about today's lesson.

Putting it all Together

So how do you juggle your mental and physical training without getting overwhelmed? Whether you are developing a mental or physical skill, the same rules apply. Keep it simple. Isolate the skill, have a plan, and practice until you develop confidence and proficiency. One of the more common mistakes many riders and other athletes make is that they underestimate the commitment needed to develop psychological skills.

For example, you may choose to begin working on your greatest weakness. If you commonly have difficulty focusing your attention, you may decide to begin working with a cue word to bring you back to your task. You then inform your trainer about this goal, so he or she can provide feedback about when they observe you to be losing your concentration. Gradually, you consciously work at bringing your attention back when you found you have lost it, and pairing this action with your cue word. Finally, you will know you are making progress toward your goal when you find your ability to refocus takes less time and mental energy. Whatever the skill, your general rule will be:

1. Isolate the skill
2. Develop a clear goal and plan
3. Inform your trainer
4. Have a way of evaluating your progress.

Developing Confidence

Confidence is a natural by-product of skill development. In assessing your own confidence level as a rider you may find variation depending upon the skill and situation. For example, one rider may have strong confidence in his ability to ride a course, but not a jump-off. Another may believe she can ride effectively, but not in the rain or other inclement weather. It is normal of course to have different confidence levels for different tasks. It may simply mean you are in the development stage of some of your skills, or be an important indicator you need to change your game plan. The rider that continually finds he cannot cope with show ring pressures is being given a very important message, which is very simply there is work to be done! How else would we know where to draw our attention, energy and resources? Confidence is also built upon a foundation of general self esteem. If you find you lack confidence in yourself in a variety of situations you may want to consider getting some outside assistance to help you boost your overall belief in yourself. Some general tips for increasing your confidence are:

Give yourself ample opportunity to experience success: Recall in our goal setting discussion that it is important to set goals that will allow you to feel successful. You can increase your chances of feeling confident if you goals are focused on process instead of outcome, and are reasonable. Goals which encourage you to extend yourself somewhat beyond your current ability are also great self esteem boosters. Goals which are too easily met often leave you feeling as though you didn't really accomplish anything worthwhile.

Prepare, prepare: If you know you have practiced adequately, you have a greater chance of feeling successful in the show ring. The rider who feels prepared can then trust themselves to let go and do the job. It is more common than you think to have that little nagging voice going off in your head berating you for not doing this or not doing that before you got to the show.

> ***Those who fail to prepare should prepare to fail***
> ***—source unknown***

Act the part: If you get to the competition and start to feel the pangs of insecurity, consider acting the part. What do you normally do when you feel confident? Are your shoulders square? Your back straight and relaxed? Do you chat with others before your class? Do you smile more? Whatever behaviours characterize confidence for you - do them. It doesn't really matter that it will feel phony at first, what may follow is a genuine return of your regard for yourself. For example, forcing yourself to smile a little more may help you to feel lighter, which may in turn produce more positive thoughts about yourself. So fake it until you make it, as they say, because you have nothing to lose!

Look for positive role models: Are there riders who possess the ability and show ring decorum you admire? If so, observe them, even interview them if you can, Find out how they got to where they are, difficult setbacks they might have faced and how they have coped with difficulty and disappointment.

Surround yourself with positive people: If someone is negative, or unsupportive of your goals, you may want to reconsider the relationship. Make sure who is around you gives you energy and confidence. If you cannot escape them, you will have to look to your focusing skills so you can block them out effectively.

Key Points:

- Learning takes conscious effort and a deliberate plan.

- Strive to be a thinking rider.

- Make sure you have a way of tracking your progress.

- Take responsibility for building your own confidence.

Chapter
9

Skills of the
Successful Competitor

When someone tells me the is only one way to do things,
it always lights a fire under my butt. My instant reaction
is, "I'm gonna prove you wrong."
—Picabo Street

Pressures Specific to Competition

Are show nerves different from 'regular nerves'? The answer is yes and no. Yes, in the sense that situations which make our butterflies roam freely in training may occur during a competition. The perfectionist is just as nervous, if not more so, in the show ring and at home. On the other hand, there are aspects of the competitive situation which create for us a whole different list of possible triggers.

Below is a list of elements that change or are different at a competition:

- your perceived level of importance of the event
- people watching you, lots of people watching you
- noise distractions: announcers, clapping
- foreign territory: including the ring, your clothes, the barn, people
- different or strange looking jumps
- multiple weather fluctuations throughout the day (especially in some places...)
- riding several times throughout the day
- changes in sleep, diet, your regular routine
- unexpected changes: your class is moved up or down, the rider before you doesn't go and you are suddenly summoned to the in-gate

Take a moment to consider situations or events which may impact the quality of your performance, and how you may cope with them should they occur, utilizing all of the skills we have covered. Within this list, you may find more opportunities to conduct simulations at home to help you cope more effectively.

Triggers which may effect my performance

Examples:
There may be so many people in my class it
feels like I don't have a chance!

My horse may be spooked by his new
surroundings, making me more nervous

_____

_____

_____

_____

_____

I'm sure you can probably come up with many more. For those who compete internationally, the list expands. Consider a new culture, language, transportation difficulties, foreign food, different rules of athlete conduct. Many Olympic athletes, their support staff and coaches will go to considerable energy thinking of possible changes or differences that may interfere with performance and ways to deal with them. I recall hearing about a hockey team traveling overseas that had to deal with a practice time of (ice time) of 1:00am. All of these things have the ability to derail us and interfere with the quality of our performance. All of these need to be considered ahead of time, and perhaps worked into your pre-competition plan.

Pre-competition Plans

Please be aware that by the time you arrive at the show ring, you should have been practicing the skills we have discussed during training in a conscientious manner. If you haven't, you will be asking yourself to do things which you are unsure of or undeveloped in your skill repertoire. A skill is an ability or proficiency that is developed over time. All the physical skills you possess as a rider you developed in training. Hopefully these skills are solid and relatively dependable. You would not expect your trainer to ask you to jump a four foot course at a competition if all you have ever jumped at home is three foot six. So don't expect that if you are nervous and tell yourself to relax and breathe, that it will be there for you. In all likelihood, it won't.

By contrast, a tool is something you use to enhance a skill. Carpenters are skilled in woodworking, and utilize tools to achieve their results. Effective riders are skilled physically and mentally, and use various tools to achieve peak performance. Each rider will ultimately use a different set of tools to reach their goals. Often some trial and error will be required to find just the right combination. One rider may use a certain cue word to refocus, another a visual image. Some will discover their best way of relaxing before a class is to listen to slow tempo music, while for others deep breathing really does the trick.

Develop your skills, experiment to find the right tools

So don't clutter up your mind with a million details at the pre-competition stage. This is where you use certain tools to get you into the right state- mind and body, to perform your best. Your plan should be short, simple and easy to execute. So how do you decide what you need to do/focus on? That depends upon what your ideal performance state is, and what you know is likely to interfere with you attaining that state most consistently. Then you will know what tools to pull from you tool box.

Knowing how you will deal with competition pressures ahead of time will mean a lot less stress

If you have been practicing the skills outlined in the beginning of this book, and observing and monitoring yourself, by this time you should have a good idea about what your ideal performance state looks like. You should also have a good understanding about what you need to do to get you into that state.

Here are a few examples:

Linda:

By observing herself at home, Linda has come to realize that she has difficulty managing her anxiety. Specifically, she has learned that her tendency toward perfectionism produces the majority of this stress. Whenever she makes a mistake, she can spend a long time recovering from it, and her self talk involves a lot of worry about how other people are judging her riding. Knowing this, Linda has focused on managing her self talk and practicing relaxation exercises daily in training. She has also made sure that her goals reflect positive and reasonable expectations of herself. At shows, Linda's pre-competition routine is this: an hour before competition she practices deep breathing exercises in order to 'bring herself down'. She then checks to make sure her self talk is focused on how she needs to ride, not how she needs to avoid mistakes. Finally, she is prepared to 'park' her mistakes should they occur, by taking a single deep breath and repeating to herself the keyword "now".

Roger:

Roger has discovered he has a bit of a 'whatever may be' personality. He cares about his riding, but often finds his way of dealing with show stress is to avoid his emotions. Consequently he often feels disconnected, or like he is "going blank". Through experimentation, Roger has learned he needs to raise his energy level in order to feel connected and focused. His pre-competition routine is this: an hour before his class, Roger listens to some upbeat music on his walk-man. He then makes sure that he interacts with others (chatting) before his class as this helps him to stay focused in the here and now. He also uses the keywords "be here" to remind him of where his focus should be.

Now describe you in your ideal performance state. You may want to now look back to the chapter on imagery and consult the ideal performance exercise.

_____

_____

_____

_____

_____

_____

Next identify some key elements, or string of elements, that will help you achieve that state. Recall what you have learned about yourself in training.

_____

_____

_____

_____

_____

_____

I never worry about falling when I'm going for a win
-Todd Brooker

After the competition

Don't just breathe a sigh of relief when your class is over, take some time to think about your performance and reflect on its strengths and weaknesses.

Consider these questions after each competition:

1.   What were your stressors for today's competition?

2.   How did you experience this stress? (Thoughts, actions, body?)

3.   How was your level of intensity (energy, being 'psyched up') for today's competition? What were your feelings at these various points?

    A. Preparing (tacking up etc.) _____   0 ·············· 5 ·············· 10
    B. Warm-up_____   **Too low   perfect   too high**
    C. Just prior to the competition_____
    D. During your competition_____

What techniques did you use to manage your stress and how effective were you at controlling it?

4.   How was your self-talk?

5.   What did you learn from today's competition that could be useful in the future (specific strategies that worked, didn't work)?

6.   What mental training techniques were most effective for you?

7.   Describe what you enjoyed about today's competition.

8.   Describe how you felt about today's competition.

The only limit to our realization of tomorrow
will be our doubts of today
-Franklin D. Roosevelt

Attributes of successful competitive riders

In my experience, I have found there are key attributes that separate the successful from the not so successful riders. To begin with, successful riders know how to manage their emotions. Being involved in sport entails dealing with stress, fear and other 'intimidating' emotions. Top athletes have trained themselves to do this effectively, like Ian Millar, who manages on a consistent basis to control all the tangle of feelings that go along with riding at the top level. Emotionally smart riders expect that in the course of training and competing they may have to deal with fear and doubt, are not afraid of them, and can even use them to create energy. They also know that they can experience an intense emotion like fear, and still perform.

Elite riders know they must move toward success, instead of 'avoid failure'. You never hear these people saying, "my goal is not to be last". This may seem absurd, but many people are in effect saying this to themselves every day, by spending a lot of energy avoiding negative events instead of moving toward positive ones. If you are actively trying to avoid negative situations, "I cannot blow this competition", this does not automatically place you on the road to success. Why? - because you are expending your energy avoiding instead of acting. Moreover, recall that you cannot visualize 'avoiding failure'.

Successful riders also know that it is about more than just winning. It is a well worn concept - the one of focusing on the journey instead of the destination, the process instead of the outcome. But it is one we could stand to remind ourselves of more. Think of all those people competing who don't see the podium, or are not seen on your TV screen for that matter. If their perception will allow, they will view themselves as accomplished. You too can have this perception if you choose.

Finally, successful riders are those who are disciplined and take responsibility. They know the value of hard work, and they do not expect anyone else to make it all happen for them. Remember you must be accountable for both your successes and your failings.

Successful riders manage their emotions, move toward success, focus on the journey and are responsible and disciplined

Key Points:

• Know what triggers can effect your performance

• Develop a simple, easily executable pre-competition plan

• Track your competition progress

About the Author

April Clay is a Chartered Psychologist residing in Calgary, Alberta, Canada. As a sport psychologist, she draws on her many years of competitive experience in show-jumping. April's articles on sport psychology for riders have appeared in Horses All, The Corinthian Horse Sport, Your Horse, Equus, Flying Changes, Horse News, New York Horse and The Eastern Equerry.

In addition to sport consulting, April specializes in blended family and divorce issues, anxiety disorders, depression, life transition and workplace issues. Her next book project, *Successful Stepmothering* is focused on how to help stepmothers negotiate their roles, and offers a special section for fathers.

If you have comments about this book, or would like to contact April:

April Clay
428, 1167 Kensington Crescent N.W.
Calgary, Alberta T2N 1X7
(403) 714-2529
email: aclay@telusplanet.net
web: www.telusplanet.net/public/aclay

April offers seminars (hourly, half day, full day) and individual assistance for riders and others on sport psychology topics. Custom seminars are available upon request, developed to suit your individual group's particular needs. Contact April at the above address for further information and pricing.

Appendix

Mental Skills Assessment:

Are you aware of what makes riding meaningful to you?

1   2   3   4   5   6   7   8   9   10

not really   very clear

How well can you set your goals and achieve them?

1   2   3   4   5   6   7   8   9   10

not very   very confident
confident in
this skill

Are you aware of what causes you stress in training and competition?

1   2   3   4   5   6   7   8   9   10

not really   very clear

Do you have strategies for managing your stress?

1   2   3   4   5   6   7   8   9   10

not very   very confident
confident in
this skill

How well are you able to visualize success?

1   2   3   4   5   6   7   8   9   10

not very   very confident
confident in
this skill

Are you aware of your self talk?

1   2   3   4   5   6   7   8   9   10

not really   very clear

Are you able to monitor and manage your self-talk?

1   2   3   4   5   6   7   8   9   10

not very   very confident
confident in
this skill

Are you aware of what kinds of situations tend to distract you from your focus?

1   2   3   4   5   6   7   8   9   10

not really   very clear

Can you concentrate under pressure filled situations?

1   2   3   4   5   6   7   8   9   10

not very   very confident
confident in
this skill

How much time do you currently devote to the mental side of your training?

1   2   3   4   5   6   7   8   9   10

not very   considerable time
much time

Bibliography

Benson, Herbert. (1975). *The Relaxation Response.* New York: Morrow.

Burns, David. (1989). *The Feeling Good Handbook.* New York: Penguin Books

Duda, J.L. (1992). Motivation in sport settings: A goal perspective approach. In G.C. Roberts (Ed.), *Motivation in sport and exercise* (pp. 57-92). Champaign, IL: Human Kinetics.

Dweck, C.S. (1986). Motivational Processes affecting learning. *American Psychologist, 41*, 1040-1048.

Ellis, A. (1982). Self direction in sport and life. Rational Living, 17, 27-33.

Langer, Ellen. (1989). *Mindfulness.* New York: Addison-Wesley Publishing

Locke, E.A. & Latham, G.P. (1990). *A theory of goal setting and task performance.* Englewood Cliffs, NJ: Prentice Hall.

Orlick, T. (1990). *In pursuit of excellence: How to win in sport and life through mental training.* Champaign, IL: Leisure Press.

Orlick, T., & Partington, J. (1988). Mental links to excellence. *The Sport Psychologist, 2,* 105-130.

Roberts, G.C. (1992). Motivation in sport and exercise: Conceptual constraints and consequence. In G.C. Roberts (Ed.), *Motivation in sport and exercise* (pp. 3-30). Champaign, IL: Human Kinetics.

Suinn, R. (1972). Removing emotional obstacles to learning and performance by visuomotor behavioral rehearsal. *Behavior Therapy, 3,* 308-310.

Taylor, J. (1996). Intensity regulation and athletic performance. In J.L. Van Raalte & B.W. Brewer (Eds.), *Exploring Sport and Exercise Psychology* (pp. 75-106).Washington, DC: American Psychological Association.

Weinburg, R.S., Burton, D., Yukelson, D., & Weigand, D. (1993). Goal setting in competitive sport: An exploratory investigation of practices of collegiate athletes. *The Sport Psychologist, 7,* 275-289.

Weinburg, R.S. (1996). Goal setting in sport and exercise: Reseach to practice. In J.L. Van Raalte & B.W. Brewer (Eds.), *Exploring Sport and Exercise Psychology* (pp. 3-24). Washington, DC: American Psychological Association.

Williams, J.M. & Leffingwell, T.R. (1996). Cognitive strategies in sport and exercise psychology. In J.L. Van Raalte & B.W. Brewer (Eds.), *Exploring Sport and Exercise Psychology* (pp.51-73). Washington, DC: American Psychological Association.

Yerkes, R.M. & Dodson, J.D. (1980). The relation of strength of stimulus to rapidity of habit formation. *Journal of Comparitive Neurology of Psychology,* 18, 459-482.

152